A Marriage Made in Italy
Area Guide 1: The Amalfi Coast

Callie Copeman-Bryant

All rights reserved. No part of the work 'A Marriage Made in Italy' may be lent, re-sold, hired or otherwise circulated, reproduced, stored in a retrieval system or transmitted on any form or by any means, electronic, mechanical, photocopying, recording, scanning or otherwise. Written permission to make a copy or copies must be obtained by the author in advance.

The right of Callie Copeman-Bryant to be identified as the author of this work has been asserted by her in accordance with the Copyright, Designs & Patents Act 1988.

Copyright © Callie Copeman-Bryant 2007

A Marriage Made Publications
www.amarriagemade.co.uk

First published 2007

ISBN: 978-1-84799-642-8

A Marriage Made and the A Marriage Made logo are trademarks.

A Marriage Made books provide independent advice and the author does not accept advertising in guide books or payment in exchange for listing or endorsing any business, or for providing positive coverage. All statements and opinions regarding businesses and locations are subjective.

The material contained herein is set out in good faith for general guidance, but no warranty can be made about the accuracy or completeness of its content. The author cannot be responsible for any errors within this work, or accept any responsibility or liability for any loss or expense incurred, or consequences arising as a result of relying on particular circumstances or statements made. Laws and regulations are complex and liable to change, and currency rates change regularly, so it is vital that readers should check the relevant legal, financial and logistical details for themselves. Details such as addresses, telephone numbers, website and email addresses are also liable to change.

Front cover image: ©Joanne Dunn Photography

Contents

The Amalfi Coast................. 3

About this Book.................. 5

Sorrento & Sant'Agnello........ 7
   Sorrento........................... 7
   Sant'Agnello..................... 9

Orientation......................... 10
   Quick Venue Guide............. 10
   Distances Matrix................. 11

Planning a Wedding in
Sorrento............................. 12

Civil Venues in Sorrento........ 13
   Cloisters of San Francesco... 14
   Convent of Santa Maria delle
   Grazie.............................. 16
   Villa Fondi........................ 17

Reception Venues in Sorrento 18
   Hotel Excelsior Vittoria......... 19
   Hotel Bellevue Syrene......... 21
   Grand Hotel Royal.............. 23
   Ristorante O'Parruchiano..... 24
   Ristorante S. Antonino......... 26
   Photo Food & Drinks........... 28

Other Recommended Hotels
in Sorrento & Sant'Agnello..... 30

How to Get There................. 31

Positano............................. 35

Orientation......................... 36
   Quick Venue Guide............. 36
   Distances Matrix................. 37

Planning a Wedding in
Positano............................. 38

Civil Venue in Positano......... 40
   Positano Town Hall............. 40

Catholic Churches in Positano 42
   Chapel of San Pietro........... 42
   Positano Cathedral............. 43

Reception Venues in Positano 44
   Covo dei Saraceni............... 44
   Palazzo Murat.................... 46
   Hotel Conca d'Oro.............. 47
   Music on the Rocks............ 49

Other Recommended Hotels
in Positano......................... 50

How to Get There................. 51

Amalfi................................ 52

Orientation......................... 54
   Quick Venue Guide............. 54
   Distances Matrix................. 54

Planning a Wedding in Amalfi. 55

Civil Venues in Amalfi........... 57
   Salone Morelli.................... 57

Catholic Churches in Amalfi... 59
   Amalfi Cathedral................. 59

Reception Venues in Amalfi.... 61
   Hotel Santa Caterina........... 61
   Hotel Luna Convento.......... 63
   EOLO/Hotel Marina Riviera... 65

Other Recommended Hotels
in Amalfi............................ 67

How to Get There................. 68

Ravello................................ 69

Orientation........................... 71
   Quick Venue Guide............. 71
   Distances Matrix................ 72

Planning a Wedding in Ravello................................ 73

Civil Venues in Ravello.......... 74
   Palazzo Tolla..................... 74

Catholic Churches in Ravello. 76
   Ravello Cathedral................ 76
   Santa Maria a Gradillo.......... 77

Reception Venues in Ravello.. 78
   Villa Cimbrone..................... 78
   Hotel Palumbo..................... 80
   Hotel Belvedere Caruso........ 82
   Albergo Ristorante Garden.... 84
   Mamma Agata..................... 86

Other Recommended Hotels in Ravello............................... 88

How to Get There................. 89

Off the Beaten Track............. 90

Local Information................. 91

Tourist Links........................ 92

White Pages – Area Contacts.. 93
   Town Halls & Churches......... 94
   Featured Reception Venues... 96
   Wedding Co-ordinators......... 98
   Photographers & Videographers..................... 100
   Ladies' Hairdressers............ 102
   Beauticians........................ 104
   Men's Hairdressers............. 105
   Florists............................. 106
   Transportation.................... 108
   Bakeries........................... 109
   Favours............................ 109
   Musicians......................... 110
   Wedding Apparel................ 111

Bibliography........................ 112

Acknowledgements............... 113

Index................................. 114

The Amalfi Coast

Plunging and dramatic, the Amalfi Coast stretches south from Naples along ragged cliffs dotted with colourful, building-block houses and hotels, descending the cliffs towards a clear, turquoise sea.

From the west-facing Bay of Naples all the way round to the east-facing Bay of Salerno, towns along this stretch might be vastly different in character but they have all retained that kind of Sophia Loren old-world class and sophistication, and all will provide a breathtaking backdrop to your wedding photos. After all, this part of the world is one of those rare places that you really don't need to visit beforehand to confirm how genuinely beautiful it is. It's not just that the photos are flattering – it really *does* look like that.

Vesuvius, the Bay of Naples & Sorrento

It is also, with good reason, the most popular area in Italy for overseas weddings, and as a bride and groom you may well feel like a tourist attraction in your own right. In fact, if you've ever wanted to know what it feels like to be a star, this is your opportunity: it's not uncommon for people here to line the streets to congratulate you, even though a wedding is not an uncommon sight.

The most popular town of all has to be Sorrento, where on some days it seems that the locals have become so used to the daily parade of brides that they have almost ceased to notice them. The town is popular for good reason: it is extremely welcoming with lots of attractions, some of the lowest prices in the area and excellent connections with all other towns and islands along the coast. It also has fabulous views of Vesuvius and experiences wonderful, dramatic sunsets – an aspect that the other towns lack, situated as they are on the east-facing side of the peninsula (although these east-facing towns do have a greater exclusivity, world-class hotels and astonishing scenery. Paradise has its downsides, however, and if the Amalfi Coast Drive doesn't give you heart failure, the price tags will).

Nearest Airport: Naples

Served by: BMI, First Choice, EasyJet, British Airways, Excel Airways, ThomsonFly

Flying time from London: Approx 2.5 hours

Best time to visit: Lent and Easter can be a rather sombre period here, but visit any time after Easter up until the beginning of June and you'll find warm weather, flowers in full bloom and not too many tourists. June to September can be uncomfortably hot and crowded (and extremely busy for weddings), but both the crowds and the temperature calm again towards the end of September and into October.

Films to get you in the mood: Only You; The Talented Mr Ripley; Marriage Italian Style; A Good Woman; Beat the Devil.

About this Book

Used in conjunction with *A Marriage Made in Italy: The Wedding Planning Guide*, this book provides you with comprehensive information and advice about getting married on the Amalfi Coast. In this particular guide you'll find an overview of logistical information, descriptions of ceremony and reception venues, and a directory of wedding related suppliers specific to the Amalfi Coast. Details of countrywide legal requirements and in-depth logistical information can be found in *The Wedding Planning Guide*, which is relevant for all locations in Italy.

Reception Venue Research

The research for the Amalfi Coast hotels and venues was carried out in from 2004 to 2007: hotels and restaurants were extensively researched to ensure that only companies with the best reviews and reputations were approached for inclusion, and all reviewed venues in this book have been personally visited and verified. Of these, the "Top Pick" venues were felt to offer the very best in the area in terms of service, location and value for money, although do bear in mind that this guide features just a selection of the venues available, and there are many other, excellent choices out there.

If you decide to research your own reception venues, use the information given for the featured venues in this guide to draft your own set of questions. Obviously you'll need to ask about basic things like deposits and timescales, but don't forget that pricing structures in Italy will be different to those in the UK. In 90% of cases, a cost quoted per head will include venue hire charges, a wedding cake and welcome drinks, so try not to compare costs per head in Italy with those in the UK where, on top of the price per head, you can expect to pay over £1000 for venue hire and around £200 for a wedding cake, for example.

Legal Requirements

As explained in Chapter 3 of *A Marriage Made in Italy: The Wedding Planning Guide*, there are very specific paperwork requirements that must be fulfilled before you can get married in Italy, and these requirements differ depending on your nationality. As in most areas, the paperwork needed for your *Nulla Osta* (the all important Italian "No Impediment" Certificate, without which the wedding can't take place) can be completed just a few months before your wedding date.

This book includes a brief outline of the steps you must take in order to fulfil the necessary requirements for ceremonies in each location, although don't forget that the rules are subject to change. **In all cases you should seek confirmation of the requirements from your tour operator, co-ordinator or consular office, and follow their guidance.** I cannot stress enough that any legal and logistical advise given in these guides must be verified, checked and double checked, or you could find your paperwork is incomplete and the marriage cannot to take place. Further information about legal requirements can be found in Chapter 3 of *The Wedding Planning Guide*.

Bride & Groom in Sorrento   ©JoAnne Dunn Photographer

Sorrento & Sant'Agnello

"When I woke up on my wedding day, the sun had already risen. There was a light mist over the sea in the bay below the hotel, and two fishermen were taking in their nets in a small, blue boat. It smelled of warm dew, and had the early-morning haze of what promised to be a good day."

Sorrento Bride

Sorrento

The hub of the area is undeniably Sorrento - a busy, bustling town where the high-pitched buzz of Vespas snake down cobbled streets filled with tiny shops and lively squares. Rising from the bay on jagged, volcanic cliffs, and so much a part of its landscape that you can't tell where the rocks end and the hotels built into the very cliff faces begin, an integral part of the charm in "the Land of the Sirens" is an atmosphere so unusual, warm and exciting that it's almost tangible. It can brush past you briefly in photos of the busy town square, but the only way it can really grab hold of you is when you immerse yourself in its life and its culture. Once you're there, you can almost feel drunk on it.

The Sorrento Coastline

A busy tourist destination with plenty of attractions of its own, the atmosphere does vary wildly from month to month. In July and August you could find yourself shoulder-to-shoulder with tourists (not to mention other brides), and the peak summer months see the emergence of such unfortunate new features as a big red open top tour bus, bars proudly serving English food, and an odd little train that trundles round the streets, Southend-style. An extremely popular wedding destination, a ceremony here can sometimes feel rather like a conveyor-belt experience; on other occasions it's clear that the locals and tourists enjoy the spectacle and do their best to make you feel special. However, if you don't fancy becoming a part of "the wedding factory" as it's rapidly becoming known, then book your wedding out of peak season - the difference will be tremendous.

In spite of all this, Sorrento has somehow managed to retain its old magic and charm, and the quieter months of April, May, September and October are particularly beautiful. It also offers plenty of ways to access the other attractions in the area, so your guests are bound to appreciate the fact that you chose a practical holiday destination. And if you like the thought of holding your wedding reception on a terrace overlooking the calm shimmering bay, sipping a glass of prosecco while the sun goes down behind Vesuvius and the warm sea breeze gently brushes the veil from your face... then this could be the place for you.

Sant'agnello

It's difficult to know where Sorrento ends and Sant'agnello begins. Certainly the main street, Corso Italia, is a more modern part of town with its own distinct character, and the area tends to be less busy than its neighbour. The hotels here are cheaper than those in Sorrento itself, and a large portion of the town is made up of various types of accommodation that house the many tourists seen trudging back and forth between the two towns during the day. Move away from the main street, however, and you'll find tiny roads that take you down to the coast or up into the lemon-groved hills and some fabulous, quiet hill-top retreats that are easily scoot-able from Sorrento itself.

Orientation

Quick Venue Guide

Size of Party	Civil Venues	Catholic Churches	Reception Venues
Up to 10	Cloisters of San Francesco Convent of Santa Maria delle Grazie Villa Fondi	None available	Hotel Excelsior Vittoria Hotel Bellevue Syrene Grand Hotel Royal O'Parruchiano S. Antonino Photo Food & Drinks
Up to 50	Cloisters of San Francesco Villa Fondi	None available	Hotel Excelsior Vittoria Hotel Bellevue Syrene Grand Hotel Royal O'Parruchiano S. Antonino Photo Food & Drinks
Up to 100	Cloisters of San Francesco Villa Fondi	None available	Hotel Excelsior Vittoria Hotel Bellevue Syrene Grand Hotel Royal O'Parruchiano S. Antonino
100+	None Available	None available	Hotel Excelsior Vittoria Hotel Bellevue Syrene Grand Hotel Royal O'Parruchiano

Distances Matrix

Ceremony Venues Reception Venues	Cloisters of San Francesco	Convent of Santa Maria delle Grazie	Villa Fondi
Hotel Excelsior Vittoria	340	210	3570
Hotel Bellevue Syrene	260	420	4170
Grand Hotel Royal	770	610	3400
Ristorante O'Parruchiano	400	480	3960
S. Antonino	190	50	3770
Photo Food & Drinks	530	350	3700

All distances are given in metres and are an approximate guide only

Planning a Wedding in Sorrento

Civil Ceremonies

Once you have followed the procedures outlined in Chapters 3 and 5 of *The Wedding Planning Guide*, you must present your documents at the Immigration Office in Naples (the *Ufficio Legalizzazioni* of the *Preffetura* at 172 Via Vespucci). Your paperwork will be authenticated by means of *bolli*, administrative stamps which you can buy from a tobacconist. Once stamped, you must take your documents to Sorrento Civil Registrar (*Ufficiale dello Stato Civile*) with an interpreter if necessary, to declare your attention to marry. Following your declaration, the banns will be posted at the Town Hall (*comune*), but you may have to wait for up to twelve days before the marriage can take place. **All these procedures will normally be handled for you by your co-ordinator or tour operator, if you have one.** For more information, see www.sorrentosposi.it/sorrentoweddings/usa.html.

Catholic Ceremonies

Unfortunately the Archdiocese of Sorrento/Castellammare recently issued a press release requesting the suspension of marriages in this area for overseas couples, a decree that affects both Sorrento and Capri. However, although this means it isn't possible for non-Italians to marry in this Archdiocese, there are many towns along the Amalfi coast that fall under the Archdiocese of Salerno where it is still possible to arrange a Catholic ceremony in several of the area's beautiful churches and cathedrals.

Other Religious (and Symbolic) Ceremonies

In Italy, only Catholic Ceremonies are considered legally binding. Other religious ceremonies may be held in any location but will be considered symbolic only. If you are planning such a wedding you must therefore also hold a civil ceremony in the UK or in Italy for your marriage to be legally binding.

Civil Venues

Civil ceremonies in Sorrento are available on all week days. More information can be found at www.comuni-italiani.it/063/080/amm.html and www.comuni-italiani.it/063/071/amm.it. Due to the language barrier it is advisable to contact them through a local co-ordinator who will also be familiar with timings, cost and logistics.

Bride & Groom in The Cloisters   *©JoAnne Dunn Photographer*

Cloisters of the Church of San Francesco

The most popular venue by far is the 13th century vaulted stone cloisters of the **Church of St Francesco (*Il Chiostro di San Francesco*).** A short walk from the main square, Piazza Tasso, The Cloisters are situated on Piazza Francesco between the main Church of St Francesco and the public gardens on the cliff-edge. They are entered by way of a narrow, stone alley that opens up into a small cloistered square with purple bougainvillea tumbling over the walls beyond – a sun-trap that's shaded by flowering plants and a tree in the centre of the quadrangle where the wedding takes place. This venue has recently experienced a huge influx of British and Irish weddings, especially since the tour operators started offering it as a destination, and in the summer it seems to be permanently set up for the ceremonies. A green aisle carpet leads you into the quadrangle, past the green plastic garden chairs set out for the guests, to a shiny, polished wooden desk where the wedding takes place, usually shaded by a large, white canopy.

It's worth noting that even though The Cloisters may be a wedding venue they are also a tourist attraction (and sometimes a make-shift art gallery) and are open to the public at all times. That means you can expect a few curious onlookers lining the walls while you pledge your life to your other half, although they do tend to be very well-behaved. For this reason it's a good idea to have music playing throughout the ceremony to muffle any noise from the uninvited guests. Besides, the acoustics here are wonderful.

Il Chiostro di San Francesco

Convent of Santa Maria delle Grazie

The **Convent of Our Lady of Graces (*Santa Maria delle Grazie*)** is a fine 17th century Palazzo situated on the busy Piazza Sant'Antonino, just a short walk from Piazza Tasso. The venue is entered through a large archway that leads from the main Piazza into a cloistered, cobbled courtyard. Its cream walls are edged with elegant, pale yellow arches, and the courtyard is filled with palm trees and colourful flower beds. Although it is difficult to see how you would fit many guests in this venue because of the layout of the garden, it does offer an alternative to the (admittedly more romantic) Cloisters, and has a slightly more formal feel. It also has the potential to offer you a little bit more exclusivity, as it is not a venue currently offered by tour operators so you're unlikely to bump into other brides there on your wedding day! A local co-ordinator can give you more information and help with bookings.

Santa Maria delle Grazie

Villa Fondi
www.pianodisorrento.net/villa_fondi.asp

A little-known hideaway in the hills of neighbouring Piano di Sorrento, Villa Fondi offers an open-air venue where you can get married in the beautiful gardens built into the cliffside, with wonderful views across the Bay of Naples towards Mount Vesuvius.

The Terrace at Villa Fondi

Piano di Sorrento is a ten-minute drive from Sorrento itself, so if your guests are staying in town you'll need to arrange transportation for the day. In peak months this venue really comes into its own; it is far less busy than the Cloisters, so if it's your dream to get married in the hot summer sun, but you want a quiet location away from the crowds, this venue should be a serious consideration.

Reception Venues

What follows is just a brief selection of reception venues covering a small variety of styles, budgets and locations. Almost all hotels and restaurants in Sorrento (of which there are plenty) will cater for wedding receptions, so you shouldn't be dissuaded from searching for your own venues. Because there is such a myriad of hotels and venues to choose from in Sorrento, it's worth knowing that the luxury ones tend to be situated on the cliff-front, which is also where the best views are.

Key to Price Guide

Please note all prices are approximate

€: Up to €50 per head
€€: €50 - €80 per head
€€€: €80 - €100 per head
€€€€: €100 - €150 per head
€€€€€: €150 - €200 per head
€€€€€€: Over €200 per head

Hotel Excelsior Vittoria €€€€€

www.exvitt.it

"No matter where I am, a warm breeze around bare shoulders will always remind me of my love for this place".

Sorrento Visitor

Choose to spend time in this world-renowned, prestigious hotel and you'll be following in the footsteps of film stars, artists and royalty – footsteps that go as far back as the early 1900s with names that include Princess Margaret, Marilyn Monroe, Sophia Loren and Enrico Caruso among the past guest list. This venue is absolutely bursting with old-world style and sophistication, and a reception here is sure to reflect that.

Ristorante Vittoria, Hotel Excelsior Vittoria

From the main square, Piazza Tasso, the gated entrance of the *Albergo Vittoria* takes you down a long, straight, tree-lined path, where dappled sunlight filters through the greenery overhead and leads you to the main body of the hotel. Aperitifs and canapés are served on a private, raised part of the terrace, situated on the cliff-edge directly opposite the looming Vesuvius, and with unbeatable views of the Sorrento coastline.

Dinner is held in the *Ristorante Vittoria*, a large, private room with rich wooden floors, opulent 18th century ceiling frescos and large windows that give unrestricted views of the terrace and the view beyond. The hotel will provide printed menus and decorate the tables with centre pieces to match your colour specification; tables are normally arranged for between six and eight people each, and the room can hold up to 60 guests.

Essential Information – Hotel Excelsior Vittoria:

Availability:	Open all year	Organisation:	A co-ordinator help you plan your event.
Size of party:	Up to 60	Entertainment:	Background accompaniment can be arranged.
Children catered for:	Yes	Exclusivity:	Only one reception would be held on the same day.

Prices from:	€160 per head.		
Price Includes			
Venue Hire	✓	Centre pieces	✗
Staff	✓	Wedding cake	✓
Meal (five courses)	✓	Entertainment	✗
Aperitifs & Canapés	✓	Table Wine	✓

Hotel Bellevue Syrene €€€€
www.bellevuesyrene.it

"The atmosphere on the Villa Pompiana terrace was incomparable. All around us were beautiful ancient frescos and mosaics while the coastline beyond was bathed in the light of the setting sun, and the dark looming beauty of Vesuvius across the bay".

Sorrento Bride

A wonderfully evocative 18th century palace built on the foundations of a Roman villa and filled with frescos and mosaics, Hotel Bellevue Syrene is a fascinating labyrinth of antique-lined corridors, comfy sitting rooms and secret, romantic suites.

Villa Pompiana Terrace, Hotel Bellevue Syrene

Two separate outdoor terraces are available for wedding receptions: for smaller parties the charming *Le Pin* Terrace, situated at the hotel entrance, looks wonderfully romantic lit up with fairy lights and can seat around 50 guests. The larger *Villa Pompiana*, with its regal Corinthian pillars and colourful mosaic floor, is tucked away at the back of the hotel and can hold up to 150 guests. In case of bad weather *Villa Pompiana* has an in-built canopy although an indoor restaurant is also available.

If you're planning on spending the night at the hotel, ask about their Honeymoon Hideaway room, a little-publicised hidden suite on the lower floors of the hotel with its own Jacuzzi cut into the rocks of the cliffs. If you're spending the night before the wedding at the hotel, *Suite Amore* has some wonderful frescos that will provide a unique background if you're planning on having photographs taken on the morning of your wedding.

This venue has spectacular, full views across the Bay of Naples and along the Sorrento coastline. The hotel is very experienced in hosting wedding receptions, and can arrange a wide selection of music and entertainment, from a simple piano accompaniment to a full Tarantella show.

Essential Information – Hotel Bellevue Syrene:

Availability:	Open all year	Organisation:	The events manager oversees the arrangement of all receptions
Size of party:	Up to 150	Entertainment:	All kinds of entertainment can be arranged, including pianists, bands, magicians and shows.
Children catered for:	Yes	Exclusivity:	Both outdoor terraces are entirely separate from one another and can be booked for exclusive use.

Prices from:	€100 per head.			
Price Includes				
Venue Hire	✓	Centre pieces	✓
Staff	✓	Wedding cake	✓
Meal (four courses)	✓	Entertainment	✗
Aperitifs & Canapés	✓		

Grand Hotel Royal €€€€
www.manniellohotels.it/royal/ukframe.html

"The best part of the day was having lunch from the extensive menu on the terrace overlooking the bay of Sorrento and Vesuvius, watching the busy ferries dashing in and out of the harbour, and the beautiful cruise ships."

Sorrento Visitor

Close to Piazza Tasso, yet in a quiet location opposite the Parco Lauro, this hotel is a cool haven of polished inlaid wood, gleaming marble floors, fresh light colour schemes and scented terrace gardens.

Relais Room, Grand Hotel Royal

Many of the cliff-front hotels in Sorrento boast wide, open terraces with similarly spectacular views, but what sets the Grand Hotel Royal apart is the wonderfully lush layout of the extra-wide terrace which is filled with tree-lined walks and little glades. This gives some added privacy as well as some much needed shade in the summer, and is a truly special place to hold a wedding reception.

Please contact the hotel for prices and details.

O'Parrucchiano €€
www.parrucchiano.com

"The waiters made such a fuss, and made us feel so special. They'd decorated the tables for us beautifully."

Sorrento Bride

Situated on Corso Italia, this popular reception venue is a remarkable structure offering possibilities for any size party. The deceptively small, dark entrance completely fails to prepare you for the startling series of tiered conservatories which open onto a beautiful, shady terrace. A popular restaurant for visiting tour groups and cruises, it lacks a sea view but is a fabulous location with a definite "wow" factor.

Terrace, Ristorante O'Parrucchiano

The restaurant has remained in the same family for 120 years and is listed among the Historical Places in Italy, having even been credited with the invention of the famous Italian dish, cannelloni. The venue is huge, and with the choice of either plant-filled conservatory rooms or a welcomingly cool, shady open terrace, it feels rather like dining in the centre of Kew Gardens: dappled sunlight filters through the leaves of the pergola, and every available space is filled with fragrant flowers and citrus trees. And all without a hint of a hanging basket in sight.

The manager is very experienced in arranging wedding receptions and, despite the size of this venue, is well able to create private, peaceful spaces among the greenery for your exclusive use, while retaining the atmosphere and geniality of a traditional family trattoria.

The restaurant has a very flexible approach to receptions, allowing you to choose or create your own set menu, or to make individual selections on the day from a wide range of excellent traditional dishes. The tables are typically set with bright white linen and sparkling wine glasses, a perfect compliment to the lush surroundings. The restaurant will also provide you with printed menus and floral centre pieces to compliment your colour scheme.

Do be warned that this venue is an *extremely* popular reception venue, and if you get married in peak season you are quite likely to be sharing it with at least one other wedding party.

Essential Information – O'Parrucchiano:

Availability:	Open all year	Organisation:	Receptions organised by restaurant manager
Size of party:	Any size	Entertainment:	Can arrange background music and musicians, including guitar and mandolin.
Children catered for:	Yes	Exclusivity:	Fully exclusive use of the restaurant is not possible and its popularity means that more than one reception may take place simultaneously, although they will be kept as separate as possible.

Prices from:	€55 per head.		
Price Includes			
Venue Hire	✓	Centre pieces	✓
Staff	✓	Wedding cake	✓
Meal (four courses)	✓	Entertainment	✗
Aperitifs & Canapés	✗		

S. Antonino €
www.weddingsorrento.com

"This was a lovely, private venue, shaded by citrus trees and flowers. The owner gave us free reign to decorate the venue and had chosen lovely linen for the tables, dotted with vases of white roses that complimented the bouquet beautifully".

Sorrento Bride

This friendly, family-run restaurant in the centre of town has a reputation for pulling out all the stops when it comes to wedding receptions, and is an absolute gem of a venue if you're looking for a traditional trattoria close to the Cloisters.

The Terrace, S. Antonino

For parties of up to 70 guests, the large shady rooftop terrace provides a relaxed, romantic setting with warm terracotta tiles underfoot and a large pergola providing a sunshade of purple bougainvilleas and citrus trees - a cool retreat from the relentless summer sun which filters down through the canopy of leaves. Although exclusive use of the terrace is not possible for smaller parties, a private area can be created for your personal use, with a team of dedicated waiting staff assigned to your party, and tables decorated with printed menus, place-cards and floral centre-pieces to match your colour scheme.

For out-of-season weddings, or in case of inclement weather, the restaurant also has an indoor dining room for up to 60 guests, featuring a brick fireplace, traditional furnishings and a colourful wall-frieze.

The dining here is as traditional as one would expect and as flexible as one could hope for: you have the choice of selecting from a range of set menus, from the à la carte (for smaller groups), or if you have something more specific in mind then the restaurant is happy to work to specific tastes, requirements and budgets.

This venue can also assist in arranging all kinds of music and entertainment, from simple background music and traditional singers, to full-scale discos and bands.

Essential Information – S. Antonino:

Availability:	Open February to December	Organisation:	Receptions organised by restaurant manager.
Size of party:	Up to 70	Entertainment:	All kinds of music can be arranged, including DJs & discos
Children catered for:	Yes	Exclusivity:	Only one wedding catered for at a time. Exclusivity of restaurant dependent on size of party. Area for reception separated.

Prices from:	€35 per head.		
Price Includes			
Venue Hire	✓	Centre pieces	✓
Staff	✓	Wedding cake	✓
Meal (four courses)	✓	Entertainment	*
Aperitifs & Canapés	✓		

*dependent on choice of entertainment

Photo Food & Drinks €
www.photosorrento.com

"Select and bring your own personal photographs that we will project on our screens during the event"

Photo Food & Drinks

"South Beach meets Amalfi Coast", summarised the diner to my left. From my right, the comment: "definite shades of Botswana", no doubt inspired by the organic place-settings and heady scent of greenery. Whatever your personal choice of metaphor, what stands out about this venue is how refreshingly different it is to the typically historical or traditional venues on offer in Sorrento. Situated close to Piazza Tasso, this cosmopolitan little venue offers a very modern touch of class, with understated décor to offset the carefully selected artwork from exhibiting photographers. The deliciously light, contemporary, freshly-cooked food with its delicate infusion of flavours offers a welcome counterbalance to the sometimes heavy pastas of the region.

Internal Restaurant, Photo Food & Drinks

This venue is small and intimate, offering you a good chance of exclusivity for your party. The indoor room of the restaurant can hold around 50 guests seated, whilst an outdoor, raised terrace can hold 70 guests for a sit-down meal, or 100 for a non-seated buffet. The terrace is relatively secluded, sheltered from the rain and the heat by a lush pergola, and dotted with comfy armchairs under wavering trees. Flexible menu options mean that all styles, budgets and formats are catered for, from formal sit-downs to informal, self-service buffets.

The manager of the restaurant can also help with sourcing suppliers for your wedding, including (and especially) photographers and videographers as well as entertainment. Within reason the tables can be decorated to your specifications, although the venue is keen to maintain its overall style; if your theme involves pink carnations, balloon arches and fussy place-settings, then you might want to think again - this is a venue for sleek column-dresses, white roses and cool, bubbling cocktails.

Essential Information – Photo Food & Drinks:

Availability:	Open all year	Organisation:	The manager of the restaurant will act as your sole point of contact, and will assist with all the arrangements.
Size of party:	Up to 70 seated, 100 standing	Entertainment:	DJ can be arranged. Dancing is permitted.
Children catered for:	Yes	Exclusivity:	In the case of larger receptions, exclusive use of both indoor and outdoor rooms. The restaurant does not cater for more than one wedding at a time.

Prices from:	€30 per head.		
Price Includes			
Venue Hire	✓	Centre pieces	✓
Staff	✓	Wedding cake	× €30
Meal	✓	Entertainment	✓
Aperitifs & Canapés	✓		

Other Recommended Hotels and Possible Reception Venues

Hotel Tramontano ★★★
www.tramontano.com

Hotel Belair ★★★
www.belair.it

Antiche Mura Hotel ★★★
www.hotelantichemura.com

Minerva Hotel ★★★ (acampora hotels)
www.acampora.it

Grand Hotel Ambasciadori ★★★
www.manniellohotels.it

Hotel Cocumella ★★★★
www.cocumella.com

Hotel La Pace ★★★★
www.ghlapace.com

Hotel Michelangelo ★★★
www.michelangelohotel.it

Hotel Meditterraneo ★★★
www.mediterraneosorrento.com

Hotel Caravel ★★★
www.hotelcaravel.com

Il Nido Hotel ★★
www.ilnido.it

La Tonnarella ★★
www.latonnarella.com

Hotel Mignon ★★
www.sorrentohotelmignon.com

Hotel Nice ★
www.hotelnice.it

Hotel Christina ★★★
www.colonnahotels.com

Hotel Alpha ★★★
www.wel.it/hotelalpha

La Pergola Hotel ★★
www.lapergolahotel.com

Hotel Angelina ★★
www.hotelangelina.it

Mama Camilla (B&B)
www.mamacamilla.com

Il Mirto Bianco (B&B)
www.ilmirtobianco.it

How to Get There

From Naples International Airport

By bus: The easiest way to get to Sorrento and Sant'agnello is by bus. Six buses a day, run by Curreri Bus Service, depart from directly outside the arrivals area of Naples Airport. The bus goes via several towns before stopping at Sant'agnello, and terminates at Piazza Tasso in the centre of Sorrento. The trip takes a little over one hour and costs around €6 per person.
Timetables can be found at www.bus.it/curreri/autolineee.htm

By train: Take a bus from Naples airport to the Napoli Centrali Station (Piazza Garibaldi). At Napoli Centrali take the stairs to the underground and head for the Circumvesuviana line. Trains to Sant'agnello and Sorrento depart every 30 minutes, take just over an hour and cost around €2.60.
See www.trenitalia.com/it/nazionali.shtml and www.vesuviana.it/infoeng.htm for more information.

By taxi: A cab from Naples airport to Sorrento via Sant'agnello will cost around €90, or if you have a small party, a minibus can be hired for around €130.

By boat: Take a bus or taxi from Naples airport to Piazza Municipio and walk to Mergellina port. There are several different hydrofoils and ferries linking Naples and Sorrento, and with a 40 minute journey it is quicker than the train or bus, although it costs double. The boats arrive at Sorrento Port, which is a steep 500m climb from the town centre. However there are shuttle buses from the Sorrento Port that run to Piazza Tasso, and buses from Piazza Tasso to take you to Sant'agnello.
See www.metrodelmare.com/inglese/home.htm and www.sorrentotourism.com/eng/ for more information.

By car: Think carefully before hiring a car here. Roads in Sorrento town centre are extremely narrow and congested, with confusing one-way systems and traffic restrictions. On top of that, the driving is particularly dangerous and parking is virtually impossible, even at the hotels. However, if you insist, the general directions are:

- turn right out of the airport and you will see the A3 in front of you
- turn right on to the main road, then left across the motorway bridge.
- turn left again and join the sliproad onto the A3, just past the Agip petrol station. This road takes you past the Naples suburbs towards Salerno.
- you should exit at Castellammare di Stabia, which will take you to the SS Sorrentine 145 - the long, winding coastal road that takes you to Sorrento through Seiano, Meta, Piano di Sorrento and Sant'agnello.

Detailed routes can be found on www.autostrade.it/en/index.html

From Rome International Airport

Another option is to fly to Rome and take the high-speed express train that connects to Naples in an hour and a half. From the main platform at Napoli Centrale, turn left and walk along the platforms until you get to the entrance for the Circumvesuviana line and the trains to Sorrento.
Timetables can be found at www.trenitalia.com/en/index.html

Getting Around

By scooter: Once you get to your destination, the coolest way to get around the area is also the most popular and the most convenient (not to mention the most fun), but you ought to have a bit of scooting experience before you try it. See page 102 for details of scooter-hire companies

©JoAnne Dunn Photographer

Positano

"Positano bites deep. It is a dream place that isn't quite real when you are there and becomes beckoningly real after you have gone."

John Steinbeck

As you travel out of Sorrento and up into the hills beyond, you begin to leave the clustered town behind, the hotels fade and the road becomes a winding ribbon, curving along the edge of the steep cliff. This is where the Amalfi Coast begins in earnest, where switchback bends take you along the impossibly steep, vertiginous mountainside, past heart-stopping drops to the sea below.

Positano appears as you come round a bend as a series of colourful, building-block houses, all stacked one on top of the other, jostling for space on the vertical incline of the mountain. If you've ever heard the phrase "you must suffer for beauty", you'll know how Positano feels; it's an astonishingly pretty place, but like most astonishingly pretty places it's also pretty impractical. Visually more dramatic than Sorrento, Positano is also more cramped and expensive, with just as many tourists but fewer attractions. If someone were to lay the town flat it would look like a game of snakes and ladders; being built on an incline might mean that it cascades romantically down towards the sea, but it also means there is no avoiding the many steep steps which take the place of streets in this town - a fact which you'll need to bear in mind if you have any less able-bodied guests or intend to invite people welded to pushchairs.

When it comes to arranging events in Positano it's more of a case of "not what you know, but who you know". I'd certainly suggest employing a middle-man to act as a buffer between yourself and the sometimes uncommunicative suppliers – a local co-ordinator will have the contacts and knowledge necessary to put the arrangements in place if it's your dream to get married in this pretty destination.

Positano

Orientation

Quick Venue Guide

Size of Party	Civil Venues	Catholic Churches	Reception Venues
Up to 10	Positano Town Hall	Chapel of San Pietro	Covo dei Saraceni Conca d'Oro Le Terrazze Palazzo Murat
Up to 50	Positano Town Hall	Chapel of San Pietro	Covo dei Saraceni Conca d'Oro Le Terrazze Palazzo Murat
Up to 100	Positano Town Hall	Positano Cathedral	Covo dei Saraceni Conca d'Oro Le Terrazze Palazzo Murat
100+	None Available	Positano Cathedral	Palazzo Murat

Distances Matrix

Ceremony Venues Reception Venues	Positano Town Hall	Chapel of San Pietro	Positano Cathedral
Covo dei Saraceni	840	2510	110
Palazzo Murat	640	2510	80
Conca d'Oro	290	2700	400
Le Terrazze	600	2480	130

All distances are given in metres and are an approximate guide only

Key to Price Guide

Please note all prices are approximate

€: Up to €50 per head

€€: €50 - €80 per head

€€€: €80 - €100 per head

€€€€: €100 - €150 per head

€€€€€: €150 - €200 per head

€€€€€€: Over €200 per head

Planning a Wedding in Positano

Civil Ceremonies

Once you have followed the procedures outlined in Chapters 3 and 5 of *The Wedding Planning Guide* and have completed the relevant wedding paperwork (available from the Italian Embassy), contact Positano Town Hall to book a provisional date, then arrange an appointment at the General Registry Office in Rome (the *anagrafe* in Via Petroselli). During this appointment you will swear an official oath (*giuramento*) and your *Nulla Osta* will be stamped with two *bolli* (stamps which you can buy from a tobacconist). Once they are stamped you must take your documents to Positano Town Hall (*comune*), with an interpreter if necessary, to declare your attention to marry. Following your declaration the banns will be posted, but you may have to wait for up to two weeks before the marriage can take place. **All these procedures will normally be handled for you by your co-ordinator or tour operator, if you have one.** For more information visit www.comuni-italiani.it/065/100/amm.it, and www.comunedipositano.it.

Catholic Ceremonies

Under Italian law, the civil and religious aspects of religious weddings are considered separate which means you must follow the civil procedure above in addition to the religious requirements. You should follow the procedures outlined in Chapters 3 and 5 of *The Wedding Planning Guide* and in addition to the documents specified, the bride and groom must provide their priest two written statements confirming their freedom to enter into the marriage. During your first meeting with the priest you will complete a pre-nuptial enquiry form and go through the details of your *pre-cana*. Following this, all documents will be submitted by the priest to the local chancery for a *Nilhil Obstat* (or *Visum Est*).

Reception Venues

It has to be said that Positano is one of the trickier locations to arrange a wedding reception in, so if you're planning the wedding yourself, make sure you call a couple of hotels and restaurants to check their availability before you set your date – and don't be surprised if your enquiry is met with a stony "non". The town is an extremely successful tourist destination and its restaurants and hotels don't want for custom – most are fully booked every night, and although the food is often excellent the customer care can sometimes leave a lot to be desired. Many venues are reluctant to cater for receptions as it restricts the influx of other customers and threatens the "exclusive" status they try hard to either attain or maintain, and if you do find a venue willing to cater for you, you may well find you have to share your dining area with other customers because of space restrictions.

Booking your wedding out of season is a good idea, although you need to bear in mind that most hotels and businesses in Positano are only open from March to November, after which the town virtually shuts down completely and the "locals" return home to Naples. Another fact to bear in mind is that, with a few exceptions, most venues in Positano do not allow dancing, so in general this location would be best suited to the smallest of wedding receptions – an intimate group table in a romantic restaurant with no more than soft music to accompany your meal.

In an attempt to avoid these restrictions, many couples hold the wedding ceremony at Positano Town Hall – taking advantage of the wedding balcony and stunning backdrop – and then move down the coast to Amalfi (consider hiring a boat and treating your guests to a champagne reception on the way) and the other venues available there.

What follows is therefore just a small selection of possible reception venues. Having searched Positano for suitable inclusions, all the venues listed here have excellent reviews, good customer service and are happy to be approached by overseas couples.

Civil Venue

Positano Town Hall

This is one of the only venues in Italy where you can hold an outdoor ceremony - the wedding hall of this bright, white building opens out onto a large, square, terracotta-tiled terrace with panoramic views high above the sea. The balcony is surrounded by splendid mountains above and to the left; to the right, Positano sweeps below and tumbles down to the boat-dotted sea. It can hold up to 60 guests (30 if seated) and is perfect in fine weather. The ornate wedding table displays a colourful depiction of the Positano panorama in hand-painted ceramic tiles, and the terrace balustrades look wonderful when festooned with flowers.

The interior of the hall holds up to 60 guests and is elegantly furnished with blue-cushioned wooden chairs. It features a grey, stone fireplace, cream walls and a floor colourfully tiled in green, blue and white ceramic. If you are one of the unlucky couples for whom the weather is not so fine, and if you have advance notice that the wedding is likely to be held inside, some floral decorations would be a good idea as the interior is fairly plain.

Wedding ceremonies are performed from Monday to Saturday, 9am – 11pm. For more information visit www.comuni-italiani.it/065/100/amm.html, or email comune@positano.campania.it.

Positano Marriage Hall (Wedding Balcony)

Positano Marriage Hall (Interior)

Catholic Churches

Chapel of San Pietro

If you're hoping for a small, intimate ceremony, then this will be a serious contender (although rumour has it that it's yet another venue in this area that will be closed to overseas couples before long, so you'll need to hurry). Covered with ivy and bougainvilleas, this tiny chapel is set high on the cliff-edge with huge glass windows overlooking the panorama of the coast. It has bright pale walls with a colourful tiled floor, beech pews, and huge, vivid paintings. Best of all if you're looking for somewhere intimate, it only has room for around 30 guests (or 40, at a squeeze). An organist can be arranged to accompany the ceremony.

San Pietro Chapel

Positano Cathedral

Situated on the lower slopes of Positano just a few minutes from the beach, the 13th century Santa Maria Assunta (Positano Cathedral) is near the centre of town, just a short walk through a pretty, flower-filled street. It is set just above beach level on a small, unremarkable piazza with sea views to the left and, if you listen very carefully, the faint sound of waves on the beach. The cathedral has a very bright baroque interior of predominantly white marble, gold accents, dark wooden pews and black and white marble tiled floors. The gold-coloured aisle and wedding chairs are set before a marble-pillared altar and the deep dome of the apse. The nave is set with chandeliers, high windows and a gold starred ceiling. Although quite cosy, the cathedral can hold up to 120 guests and performs ceremonies in English. It is also possible to arrange an organist and singers for the ceremony.

Positano Cathedral

Reception Venues

Hotel Covo dei Saraceni €€€
www.covodeisaraceni.it

"It's hard to find a more romantic location - sitting on the terrace restaurant under the stars being serenaded on the piano was heavenly"

Positano Honeymooner

This five-star hotel is situated on a beach-level outcrop very close to the Cathedral, so while it doesn't have the dizzyingly high terrace panoramas of many other Amalfi Coast hotels, it does have one of the most enviable positions in Positano. Its ocean-facing terraces look out over dozens of tiny boats, all to the soothing soundtrack of waves washing the sand.

Restaurant Savino, Hotel Covo dei Saraceni

The hotel has two restaurants available for wedding receptions. The indoor restaurant, where vines climb across the white-washed walls and ceiling, has sea views and can hold up to 250 guests, although it can be sectioned-off with trees and plants for the use of smaller parties. The second restaurant, situated on the sea-facing terrace under a shady pergola, holds 40 guests. Guitar and mandolin music can be arranged.

Essential Information – Covo dei Saraceni:

Availability:	Open mid-March to early January.	Organisation:	The manager of the hotel will act as your point of contact, and will assist with all the arrangements.
Size of party:	Up to 250	Entertainment:	Soft background music, piano or guitar
Children catered for:	Yes	Exclusivity:	On some occasions, more than one reception may be catered for at the same time, although these will be kept separate on different floors and will only occur when the groups are very small.

Prices from:	€80 per head.			
Price Includes				
Venue Hire	✓	Centre pieces	✗	
Staff	✓	Wedding cake	✓	
Meal (five courses)	✓	Entertainment	✗	
Aperitifs & Canapés	✗			

Hotel Palazzo Murat €€€€
www.palazzomurat.it

"The evening reception was like a magical garden fairy tale amongst the beautiful plants and trees, with the vine grown archway dimly lit by candles and soft relaxing music."

Positano Bride

This 18th century baroque palazzo hotel in the centre of Positano features a wonderful, multilevel botanical garden in which you can host your evening reception, and even hold a symbolic ceremony. Receptions are held in the hotel's garden restaurant, *al Palazzo*, where tables are set among the greenery.

Garden Restaurant, Hotel Palazzo Murat

The courtyard here, *il Patio*, is also used as a venue for classical music recitals; in fact, only classical music is permitted at the Murat - definitely something to bear in mind when you're arranging your reception music. This is a very different option from the usual sea-facing terrace venues – it offers a wonderfully secluded location, surrounded by tropical plants, banana trees, and the heady scent of a hundred flowers.

Please contact the venue for prices and details.

Hotel Conca d'Oro €€€
www.hotel-concadoro.com

"I can't say enough good things about the Conca D'Oro... everything was fine-tuned to the last detail and was just perfect, and the view is unforgettable when you reach the reception area."

Positano Bride

This quiet and friendly venue is situated slightly out of the town centre, very close to Positano Wedding Hall, and reached by climbing an asthma-inducing 150 steps. There's no other access to the hotel so it's inadvisable if you have any less able-bodied guests, but bear in mind this *is* Positano, so the snakes and ladders theme is par for the course in this area.

Once you get there, however, you'll find an oasis of calm and a friendly welcome that can be hard to find elsewhere in this part of the Amalfi Coast. The hotel staff are extremely enthusiastic about assisting with all arrangements, and this is sure to make the organisation a pleasure. Receptions are held on a charming, sea-view sun terrace which is used both for the meal, and for music and dancing in the evening. A variety of buffets or sit-down menus can be created to the couple's specifications, with the reputedly excellent food all sourced from local produce.

This is a great venue for couples on a budget, as it offers some excellent value for money in a notoriously expensive town.

Essential Information – Conca d'Oro:

Availability:	Open mid-March to early January.	Organisation:	The hotel will assist you in all arrangements, including flowers, booking of the Town Hall, the reception, music and all transfers, hairdressing, beauty services and photographers. This venue is also able to arrange fireworks if required.
Size of party:	Up to 100	Entertainment:	The hotel can arrange either a band (jazz, pop or Italian music), or guitar and mandolin. Music and dancing permitted until midnight.
Children catered for:	Yes	Exclusivity:	Only one wedding will be catered for at a time.

Prices from:	€80 per head.		
Price Includes			
Venue Hire	✓	Centre pieces	✗
Staff	✓	Wedding cake	✓
Meal (five courses)	✓	Entertainment	✗
Aperitifs & Canapés	✓		

Music on the Rocks
www.musicontherocks.it

Situated right underneath Le Terrazze Restaurant, yet somehow managing not to impinge upon it at all, is Music on the Rocks; a friendly, quaint nightclub built into the cliffs, offering the perfect way to round off your wedding reception if you can't resist a boogie. Be aware that both Le Terrazze and Music on the Rocks are popular with bridal parties because of their proximity to one another, so in peak months you're more than likely to see a few other white dresses around.

Whilst you can't actually hold a wedding reception here at the club, I've featured it for those couples who are planning receptions in any of the local restaurants and are looking for somewhere to dance the night away afterwards. Alternatively, this would make an excellent hen or stag night option.

Other Recommended Hotels and Possible Reception Venues

Eden Roc Suites Hotel ★ ★ ★
www.edenrocpositano.com

Hotel Marincanto ★ ★ ★ ★
www.marincanto.it

Hotel Villa Franca ★ ★ ★ ★
www.villafrancahotel.it

Albergo Miramare ★ ★ ★ ★
www.miramarepositano.it

Hotel Poseidon ★ ★ ★ ★
www.hotelposeidonpositano.it

Hotel Buca di Bacco ★ ★ ★ ★
www.bucadibacco.it

Ristorante Le Terrazze
www.leterrazzerestaurant.it

Casa Albertina ★ ★ ★
www.casalbertina.it

Hotel California ★ ★ ★
www.hotelcaliforniapositano.it

Hotel Pupetto ★ ★ ★
www.hotelpupetto.it

Maria Luisa ★
www.pensionemarialuisa.com

Villa Nettuno ★
www.villanettunopositano.it

Villa Fiorentino

How to Get There

From Naples International Airport

By car: Follow the directions to Sorrento, then take the SS145 coastal road. Be aware that the Amalfi Coast Drive is extraordinarily beautiful but very dangerous. You'll need to be an experienced, skilled driver, and even then the combination of road width (or lack of it), switchback bends and the antics of other drivers can prove a perilous challenge. Total journey time from Naples is 1 hour 30 minutes. Parking in the town is virtually non-existent. Detailed routes can be found on www.autostrade.it/en/index.html

By bus: Use the Curreri bus to get to Sorrento (see page 31). SITA buses run from Sorrento to Viale Pasitea in Positano.
SITA bus timetables can be found at www.sitabus.it/wps/portal/OrariCampania

By ferry: Use the Curreri bus to get to Sorrento (see page 31), and take the shuttle bus from Piazza Tasso to Sorrento Port. Ferries run in peak season only. For timetables visit www.amalficoastweb.com/amalfi/english/amalfi_coast_ferries.html

Amalfi

"...here on a cliff overlooking the Tyrrhenian Sea, a view unchanged since Ulysses, as usual off course, came floating by millennia ago."

Gore Vidal

Leaving Positano behind, the coastal road continues its perilous journey around the cliff side before sweeping down towards the Byzantine naval town of Amalfi. Somewhat less whimsical than the poetic Positano and Ravello but with more heavyweight art and history, the town is wedged into a tiny cove and, with a population of 5,000, is by far the largest along the coast. After Sorrento, it offers visitors the most in terms of attractions and accessibility.

Overlooking the Bay of Salerno, Amalfi is a friendly town dominated by the disproportionately large *duomo*. It spreads out in all directions via narrow alleyways and open courtyards to tree-lined paths that navigate the steep hills beyond. Relatively quiet out of peak season, the summer months see it busy with the tourists who stay in the town itself or visit on day trips from the other towns and villages along the Amalfi Coast.

Amalfi

Amalfi is one of the more tourist-friendly towns along the coast. It offers plenty of attractions of its own, and provides regular connections by bus and boat to Positano, Ravello, Sorrento, Naples and the islands of Capri & Ischia. Also nearby are the much less touristy towns of Praiano and Atrani - handy if you fancy a slightly "off the beaten track" experience.

Coming as it does after Positano, Amalfi tends to get rather a scant deal when it comes to weddings. Situated between two such startlingly lovely places as Positano and Ravello, Amalfi is in danger of looking rather ordinary at first glance. The town centre simply doesn't have the dramatic, cliff-top views and the town layout isn't as quirkily breathtaking. Like Positano, the town is centred on its sea-level port, but it doesn't wriggle off up into the mountains in quite the same way. There's a lot to be said for this as, with the exception of the steep cathedral steps, the location is relatively flat – a distinct advantage when you consider you could be overheating in a heavy wedding dress with your make-up about to slide off your face.

If you do get the chance to visit Amalfi, don't just dismiss it out of hand because of the visual overload you experienced on the way round. Take the time to have a cup of coffee and let the atmosphere sink in for a while. Once you've spent a small amount of time in here you'll see that it's not too dissimilar to Sorrento, with similar accessibility and a wider range of options than its immediate neighbours. For that reason, don't overlook it – the inhabitants are welcoming and friendly, and a wedding here would have far greater exclusivity than you'd achieve on some other parts of the coast.

Orientation

Quick Venue Guide

Size of Party	Civil Venues	Catholic Churches	Reception Venues
Up to 10	Salone Morelli	Amalfi Cathedral	Ristorante EOLO Hotel Santa Caterina Hotel Luna Convento
Up to 50	Salone Morelli	Amalfi Cathedral	Ristorante EOLO Hotel Santa Caterina Hotel Luna Convento
Up to 100	Salone Morelli	Amalfi Cathedral	Hotel Santa Caterina Hotel Luna Convento
100+	None Available	Amalfi Cathedral	Hotel Santa Caterina Hotel Luna Convento

Distances Matrix

Ceremony Venues Reception Venues	Salone Morelli	Amalfi Cathedral
Hotel Santa Caterina	1090	960
Hotel Luna Convento	300	400
EOLO/Marina Riviera	140	240

All distances are given in metres and are an approximate guide only

Planning a Wedding in Amalfi

Civil Ceremonies

Once you have followed the procedures outlined in Chapters 3 and 5 of *The Wedding Planning Guide* and have completed the relevant wedding paperwork (available from the Italian Embassy), contact Amalfi Town Hall to book a provisional date, then arrange an appointment at the General Registry Office in Rome (the *anagrafe* in Via Petroselli). During this appointment you will swear an official oath (*giuramento*) and your *Nulla Osta* will be stamped with two *bolli* (stamps which you can buy from a tobacconist). Once they are stamped you must take your documents to Amalfi Town Hall (*comune*), with an interpreter if necessary, to declare your attention to marry. Following your declaration the banns will be posted, but you may have to wait for up to two weeks before the marriage can take place. **All these procedures will normally be handled for you by your co-ordinator or tour operator, if you have one.**

For more information visit www.comuni-italiani.it/065/006/amm.html.

Catholic Ceremonies

See the information on page 38 for information on how to arrange Catholic Ceremonies.

Reception Venues

Hotels and restaurants in Amalfi are incredibly welcoming and all seem happy to be approached as reception venues. Because of the proximity of the Positano Wedding Balcony and the relative austerity of the Amalfi Town Hall, it is a less popular choice of location, at least for civil ceremonies. However, if you're holding a civil ceremony in Positano and are having trouble arranging a reception venue there, you'll find the hotels and restaurants in Amalfi will be happy to help.

View of Amalfi from Ristorante EOLO

Key to Price Guide

Please note all prices are approximate

€: Up to €50 per head

€€: €50 - €80 per head

€€€: €80 - €100 per head

€€€€: €100 - €150 per head

€€€€€: €150 - €200 per head

€€€€€€: Over €200 per head

Civil Venue

Salone Morelli

Situated behind Positano Cathedral, Salone Morelli (5 Piazza Municipio) is a 12th Century Benedictine Monastery and the most ancient marriage hall in Italy. Overlooking the ocean it has a distinctly medieval feel, with a beautiful tiled floor and dark polished wooden tables. If you're an art buff then this venue may offer an added interest as it houses paintings by Domenico Morelli and Pietro Scoppetta. Photo opportunities near the *Salone* include the palazzo outside the *duomo* and the 13th century Arabian-style *Il Chiostro di Paradiso* with their ancient sarcophagi, marble sculptures and mosaics. The ceremony is conducted in Italian and the venue can hold up to 70 guests.

Salone Morelli

Il Chiostro di Paradiso – the Paradise Cloisters – perfect for wedding photos

Catholic Churches

Amalfi Cathedral

You can't picture Amalfi without picturing its incredible, black and white *duomo* in the heart of the town. Dating from the 10th century, The most notable features of St Andrew's Cathedral are its steep steps and striped mosaic facade. Inside you'll find marble pillars and high vaulted, frescoed ceilings. The ceremony is usually held in Italian by the Priest of Amalfi and can be accompanied by an organist and choir. Don't worry about capacity – this place is huge, although do bear in mind that the cathedral is a major tourist attraction so you might find your wedding has a few onlookers. If you're planning a smaller ceremony you should consider one of the smaller side alters which offer rather more intimacy.

Amalfi Cathedral – Central Nave

Amalfi Cathedral – Side Altar

There is also a little-known private chapel in Amalfi which is part of Hotel Luna Convento. Hire of this chapel would have to be arranged through the Hotel of course, and you'd need to arrange for a priest to conduct the ceremony.

Reception Venues

Hotel Santa Caterina €€€€€€
www.hotelsantacaterina.it

"The service impeccable, and the hotel's pool, outdoor restaurant, and lemon groves are like a dream."

Amalfi Honeymooner

Many of the five star hotels along the Amalfi coast boast an impressive past guest list, with evocative names from Hollywood's golden age lending an impression of timeless glamour. This may be one such hotel, but from the look of their recent guest list the Hollywood glamour has pervaded and you'll be following in the footsteps of the likes of Brangelina if you choose this venue. The first restaurant is in the main body of the 19th century hotel, which is situated just outside Amalfi, high above sea-level and dominating extensive grounds. With space for up to 100 guests, bright marble floors, and ivy climbing the white-washed walls, the expansive windows of this restaurant open out onto a terracotta tiled terrace which looks down past the grounds towards the sea.

Below the hotel, terraces lead down to the sea in a series of citrus groves and Mediterranean gardens. At sea-level you will find the second, more rustic open-air *Ristorante Al Mare* which overlooks the coast beyond and is perfect for smaller, summer parties. Soft music only is permitted at this venue.

Essential Information:

Availability:	Open March to December	Organisation:	The point of contact is the manager of the hotel, who will oversee all arrangements
Size of party:	Up to 170	Entertainment:	Mandolin, saxophone and piano accompaniments can be arranged and are available up to 11.45pm
Children catered for:	Yes	Exclusivity:	On most occasions only one wedding will be catered for at a time. In the case of small weddings, two may be catered for but will be held in separate parts of the hotel

Prices from:	€230 per head.		
Price Includes			
Venue Hire	✓	Centre pieces	✓
Staff	✓	Wedding cake	✓
Meal (four courses)	✓	Entertainment	✗
Aperitifs & Canapés	✓		

Music available for around €800

Hotel Luna Convento €€€€
www.lunahotel.it

"As dusk fell and the candles glowed around us, we gazed out across the town of Amalfi and the tiny villages beyond, as the coast line lit up in the dying light of a perfect evening."

Amalfi Bride

Torre Restaurant

This highly professional and very experienced venue is a sympathetically converted 13th century convent, whose past guests (Humphrey Bogart, Ingrid Bergman and Simone de Beauvoir, to name but a few) lay testament to its stylish charm. Situated on the cliff-front close to the centre of the town, Hotel Luna Convento is extremely well appointed to cater for weddings and is sure to knock the socks off your guests. The service here is excellent, with the hotel owner giving truly personal attention to each wedding.

Among its unusual features, the hotel has its own private chapel which can be booked for the ceremony. The secluded chapel holds around 50 guests, has wonderful white marble arches and 13th century frescos and, rather unusually, offers both Catholic and Protestant ceremonies. An organist is available along with a violinist & choir.

Leading from the chapel at mid-level is a pretty, cloistered courtyard, perfect for serving welcome drinks among the orange and lemon trees before your guests are escorted across the road to the summit of a private, open-air restaurant situated on top of a Saracen watchtower with fabulous panoramic views and room for up to 40 guests. As an added draw, the top of the tower has recently been converted into a fabulous, circular honeymoon suite.

A second restaurant is available for larger parties, with room for up to 120 guests and with the kind of uninterrupted, panoramic views that could fool you into thinking you were on board a cruise ship rather on terre-ferme. As Simone de Beauvoir commented, "I would have stayed a long time on the terrace looking at the ships' lights shining on the silky sea".

Essential Information:

Availability:	Open all year	Organisation:	The point of contact is the manager of the hotel, who will oversee all arrangements
Size of party:	Up to 150	Entertainment:	Soft background music is permitted in the main body of the hotel. Receptions in the Tower restaurant can host live music and dancing.
Children catered for:	Yes. Evening entertainment for children can be arranged	Exclusivity:	Only one reception will be catered for at a time

Prices from:	€120 per head.			
Price Includes				
Venue Hire	✓	Centre pieces	✗	
Staff	✓	Wedding cake	✓	
Meal (four courses)	✓	Entertainment	✗	
Aperitifs & Canapés	✓			

Ristorante Eolo (and Hotel Marina Riviera) €€€
www.marinariviera.it/eolo

"Ours was a small scale budget friendly wedding, with the reception at Eolo Ristorante and wonderful views of the ocean and the town."

Amalfi Bride

I wouldn't normally feature two different venues in this way, but these two complement each other so well that it seems a shame not to. Co-owned but operating independently, together these two venues offer you a fabulous setting for pre and post wedding drinks, and an extremely well-regarded restaurant for your reception meal.

Ristorante EOLO

Ristorante EOLO may not quite be open-air, but it does have wonderfully large, arched windows overlooking the sea. A small, intimate venue, it can cater for up to 40 guests in understated, elegant surroundings, and offers some of the best food I've ever tasted in this area. The service is excellent and abounds with special touches; a reception held here would without doubt be given the special attention it deserves.

Situated next door, Hotel Marina Riviera is a converted villa and would provide excellent accommodation if you use EOLO for your reception. The suites have wonderfully spacious balconies - useful for when you and your bridesmaids need that extra space to get ready. The hotel owners are extraordinarily welcoming and helpful, and would liaise with the restaurant to help you co-ordinate your arrangements and requirements for the day.

Please contact the restaurant for prices and details.

Other Recommended Hotels and Possible Reception Venues

Miramalfi ★★★
www.miramalfi.it

Hotel Lidomare ★★★
www.lidomare.it

Floridiana Hotel ★★★
www.hotelfloridiana.it

Hotel Centrale ★★★
www.hotelcentraleamalfi.it

Ristorante La Caravella
www.ristorantelacaravella.it

Hotel Fontana ★★★
www.hotel-fontana.it

Hotel Antica Repubblica Amalfi ★★★
www.starnet.it/anticarepubblica

Hotel Amalfi ★★★
www.starnet.it/hamalfi

Villa Lara Hotel ★
www.villalara.it

How to Get There
From Naples International Airport

By car: Follow the directions to Sorrento, then take the SS145 coastal road. Be aware that the Amalfi Coast Drive is extraordinarily beautiful but very dangerous. You'll need to be an experienced, skilled driver, and even then the combination of road width (or lack of it), switchback bends and the antics of other drivers can prove a perilous challenge. Total journey time from Naples is 2 hours 30 minutes.
Detailed routes can be found on www.autostrade.it/en/index.html

By bus: SITA busses run directly to Amalfi from Naples 7 times a day, and from Salerno 3 times a day.
To reach Amalfi via Sorrento, use the Curreri bus to get to Sorrento (see page 31) and take the SITA bus from Piazza Tasso to Piazza Flavio Gioia, which runs via Positano 12 times a day.
SITA bus timetables can be found at www.sitabus.it/wps/portal/OrariCampania

By ferry: In peak season, ferries connect Amalfi with Sorrento, Naples, Salerno, Positano, Ischia and Capri.
For timetables visit
www.amalficoastweb.com/amalfi/english/amalfi_coast_ferries.html

Ravello

"Ravello is nearer to the sky than it is to the shore"

André Gide

Continuing on from Amalfi, the coastal road rises steeply inland towards Ravello and the most spectacular views of them all. 350 metres above sea level, this vertigo-inducing town has an impressive cultural history and has attracted a wealth of writers, composers and celebrities throughout the years. With its bright white houses, cobbled alleyways and terraced landscape, it is especially attractive in the evenings when the day-trippers have gone home. A wedding reception here among the many gardens and quiet squares would be a more private experience than the other towns along the coast would offer.

Ravello is an astonishing place. It's calm, it's magical and it has to be the most beautiful town in the area. Luckily it's pretty much left alone by most tourists who do descend on the place during the day but tend to leave it in peace in the evenings. Apart from the *duomo* in the town square, the other venues are tucked away slightly and so it's well situated if you want a peaceful wedding away from the hubbub of the tourist crowds.

View from Ravello

Whilst it is undoubtedly the most romantic, peaceful spot in the area but of course, like everywhere, it does have its down sides: it seems to take an age to get anywhere else for one thing, and aside from the admittedly marvellous view and extremely relaxing atmosphere, there isn't really much else to see. Your guests might find it somewhat restrictive if they are planning to spend more than a few days there or wish to tour the area, so if you suspect they'd appreciate something more than a quiet, uneventful getaway, it may be worth recommending that they book a night or two in Ravello and spend the rest of their stay in nearby Amalfi, which has good transport links to the other tourist attractions in the area.

Weddings here are popular, but not so much that you'll feel part of a conveyor belt experience by any means. It's still a good idea to hire a wedding co-ordinator as Ravello is a good two hour drive from Naples airport, so quick trips over to co-ordinate things yourself could get a little tiresome.

Orientation

Quick Venue Guide

Size of Party	Civil Venues	Catholic Churches	Reception Venues
Up to 10	Palazzo Tolla	Santa Maria a Gradillo	Ristorante Garden Villa Cimbrone Hotel Palumbo Hotel Caruso Belvedere Mamma Agata
Up to 50	Palazzo Tolla	Santa Maria a Gradillo	Ristorante Garden Villa Cimbrone Hotel Palumbo Hotel Caruso Belvedere
Up to 100	None available	Santa Maria a Gradillo Ravello Cathedral	Villa Cimbrone Hotel Palumbo Hotel Caruso Belvedere
100+	None available	Santa Maria a Gradillo Ravello Cathedral	Villa Cimbrone Hotel Palumbo Hotel Caruso Belvedere

Distances Matrix

Ceremony Venues Reception Venues	Palazzo Tolla	Santa Maria a Gradillo	Ravello Cathedral
Villa Cimbrone	760	760	580
Hotel Palumbo	30	160	190
Hotel Belvedere Caruso	110	130	260
Ristorante Garden	320	320	140
Mamma Agata	770	770	550

All distances are given in metres and are an approximate guide only

Key to Price Guide

Please note all prices are approximate

€: Up to €50 per head

€€: €50 - €80 per head

€€€: €80 - €100 per head

€€€€: €100 - €150 per head

€€€€€: €150 - €200 per head

€€€€€€: Over €200 per head

Planning a Wedding in Ravello

Civil Ceremonies

Once you have followed the procedures outlined in Chapters 3 and 5 of *The Wedding Planning Guide* and have completed the relevant wedding paperwork (available from the Italian Embassy), contact Ravello Town Hall to book a provisional date, then arrange an appointment at the General Registry Office in Rome (the *anagrafe* in Via Petroselli). During this appointment you will swear an official oath (*giuramento*) and your *Nulla Osta* will be stamped with two *bolli* (stamps which you can buy from a tobacconist). Once they are stamped you must take your documents to Ravello Town Hall (*comune*), with an interpreter if necessary, to declare your attention to marry. Following your declaration the banns will be posted, but you may have to wait for up to two weeks before the marriage can take place. **All these procedures will normally be handled for you by your co-ordinator or tour operator, if you have one.**

For more information visit www.comuni-italiani.it/065/104/amm.html.

Catholic Ceremonies

See the information on page 38 for information on how to arrange Catholic Ceremonies.

Reception Venues

Ravello is quite a popular destination for stars, celebrities, media bigwigs and big cheeses in business, and the service here reflects that. In contrast to the nouveau stuffiness you can find in some of the other towns, the staff here tend to be extremely friendly but polite, and the atmosphere is relaxed but impeccable. Unlike some of the other towns which practically close out of season, in Ravello several venues will offer you the opportunity to book for your exclusive use between the months of November and March.

Civil Venue

Palazzo Tolla

Situated in the centre of the town near the gardens of Villa Rufolo is the 12th century Palazzo Tolla at Ravello Town Hall (1 Via San Giovanni del Toro). A pretty, pergola-shaded path leads you to the hall, which is entered through an arch that opens out onto the gardens beyond. Ceremonies can be performed either in the garden area with its views of the town, or within the hall itself - a splendid room with a dark, terracotta tiled floor, white walls decorated with plenty of paintings, and a gleaming, polished wooden desk at which the ceremony takes place. This is a fairly small venue that can hold up to 40 guests, and can be booked for any day of the week.

Palazzo Tolla interior

Entrance to Palazzo Tolla

Catholic Churches

Ravello Cathedral

Situated on the large pedestrianised square is Ravello Catherdral, a large, white 12th century baroque building. Fairly sparse in comparison to the other *duomi* in the area, the interior has an elegance that is befitting to the location, with white marble vaulted arches and pillars, and just the odd touch of opulence. The cathedral holds up to 120 guests and is available any day of the week. The mass can be conducted in English, and accompanied by organists and sopranos.

Ravello Cathedral

Santa Maria a Gradillo

A more intimate venue is the somewhat smaller S. Maria a Gradillo, close to the central piazza and with room for up to 70 guests. This is a much plainer church, but elegant nonetheless, with two aisles and beautifully carved marble columns.

Santa Maria a Gradillo

Reception Venues

Villa Cimbrone €€€€€
www.villacimbrone.it

"Villa Cimbrone is the top of the tree in Ravello for a wedding venue"

Ravello Groom

This old Roman villa is situated 10 minutes walk from the centre of the town, approached by steep steps in an area sufficiently secluded for Greta Garbo when she famously wanted to be alone, and DH Lawrence while penning the controversial *Lady Chatterley's Lover*.

The hotel has many interesting features including the extensive, landscaped public gardens with their temples, grottos and ancient cloisters, where Protestant, Jewish and symbolic ceremonies can also be held. There are many possibilities for receptions which can be held on panoramic terraces, inside the villa, outside in the gardens or in the atmospheric, vaulted crypt. It also has the advantage of allowing dancing and any kind of music until midnight.

Essential Information:

Availability:	Open all year, but available from 6pm only	Organisation:	This venue has a dedicated wedding co-ordinator and assistant
Size of party:	Up to 140	Entertainment:	Every kind of entertainment can be arranged from string quartets and guitar accompaniments, to jazz bands and DJs. Dancing permitted until midnight
Children catered for:	Yes.	Exclusivity:	Only one reception will be catered for at a time

Prices from:	€200 per head.		
Price Includes			
Venue Hire	✓ *	Centre pieces	✓
Staff	✓	Wedding cake	✓
Meal (four courses)	✓	Entertainment	✗
Aperitifs & Canapés	✓	Coffee & Liquers	✓

*There is an additional charge to use the Belvedere Terrace

Hotel Palumbo €€€€
www.hotel-palumbo.it

"An elegant and comfortable five-star hotel converted from another old palazzo, with astonishing views of both the mountains and sea from its terrace and an atmosphere of civilised calm".

David Lodge

This hotel, with its wonderful ceiling frescos and antiques, is in an ideal location if you are holding a civil ceremony as it is situated right opposite the Town Hall and is therefore well used to catering for wedding receptions. The hotel's past guests include Tenessee Williams and Amedeo Modigliani, and it has even seen Richard Wagner trying out his new tunes on the family piano.

Receptions can be held in the opulent dining rooms, *Sala Grande* and *Sala San Giovani*, which hold up to 150 people. For smaller parties, the vine covered dining terrace with its view of Littari Mountains, vineyards and brilliant blue ocean holds up to 30 guests. The villa is famed for the terraced garden overlooking what Gore Vidal described as "the most beautiful view in the world", and which offers yet another option for up to 250 guests. This wonderfully flexible venue also offers both outdoor and indoor Protestant and symbolic ceremonies.

Essential Information:

Availability:	Open all year	Organisation:	The manager of the hotel offers a very personal service and will take care of the arrangements
Size of party:	Up to 160	Entertainment:	On application
Children catered for:	Yes.	Exclusivity:	

Prices from:	€140 per head.			
	Price Includes			
Venue Hire	✓	Centre pieces	✓
Staff	✓	Wedding cake	✓
Meal (four courses)	✓	Entertainment	✗
Aperitifs & Canapés	✓		

Hotel Caruso Belvedere €€€€€
www.hotelcaruso.com

"If you are thinking of pushing the boat out, the Caruso is the place"

Ravello Visitor

Another favourite of celebrities past and present, this 11th century palace with its hanging gardens 1000ft above sea level has several options for wedding receptions.

The main restaurant, *Ristorante Caruso,* with its wonderful arches and sea views seats up to 80 people. It has direct access to a wonderful garden which is the setting for the second restaurant, *Belvedere,* which can seat up to 120 guests and is one of the only venues with a 360º view of the coast and surrounding landscape. Also available are two conference rooms, *Wagner* and *Colonne* both of which are available for receptions. They hold up to 120 guests each, or can be combined to provide one room for larger parties.

Essential Information:

Availability:	Open March to November	Organisation:	The PR Manager will work with the Food & Beverage Manager to organise your reception
Size of party:	Up to 200	Entertainment:	Very high quality musicians can be arranged, including pianist, singer, violinist, harpist, mandolin & guitarists. A Tarantella group can also be organised.
Children catered for:	Yes. Babysitters can be provided if required.	Exclusivity:	Only one wedding is catered for at a time

Prices from:	On application.		
Price Includes			
Venue Hire	✓	Centre pieces	✓
Staff	✓	Wedding cake	✓
Meal (four courses)	✓	Entertainment	✗
Aperitifs & Canapés	✓		

*Entertainment for approximately €200

Albergo Ristorante Garden €€
www.hotelgardenravello.it

"The Garden Restaurant has magnificent views of the Amalfi Coastline, and after sunset you feel as if you are dining in the clouds".

Ravello Visitor

Once visited by Jackie O and apparently frequented by Gore Vidal, this restaurant offers an open-air, cliff top terrace in garden surroundings, situated in the centre of Ravello and bordering the stunning gardens of Villa Rufolo. It offers the choice of a wide, vine-covered terrace or a large, glass-fronted dining room, both overlooking the coast and surrounding mountains.

Essential Information:

Availability:	Open March to November	Organisation:	The manager of the hotel will handle arrangements
Size of party:	Up to 90	Entertainment:	All kinds of music can be arranged, including classical, jazz and DJ. Dancing is permitted.
Children catered for:	Yes	Exclusivity:	Only one wedding is catered for at a time

Prices from:	€50 per head		
Price Includes			
Venue Hire	✓	Centre pieces	✓
Staff	✓	Wedding cake	✓
Meal (four courses)	✓	Entertainment	✗
Aperitifs & Canapés	✗		

Mamma Agata €€€€
www.mammaagata.com

"A wedding at Mamma Agata's home is a truly unforgettable experience and a memory we will treasure forever".

Ravello Bride & Groom

This is an exceptionally special place. Situated just outside Ravello, Mamma Agata is a real foodies' heaven run by a native of the town who has cooked for many of the past Hollywood greats (a list that includes Humphry Bogart, Richard Burton, Elizabeth Taylor and Fred Astaire, among others). The food here is as sublime as you'd expect it to be, yet is served in a rustic, homely setting.

Mamma Agata is generally run as a cooking school, which can add a fabulous dimension to your wedding. As an added extra, and to give an unforgettably personal touch, how about holding your hen night here as you help to prepare your own wedding feast?

The family here adore weddings and work extremely hard to make your day extra special. Working closely with you, Mamma Agata's English-speaking daughter Chiara will liaise with you and local suppliers to ensure the food and the décor match your requirements perfectly.

This is an excellent option if you want a homely Italian feel to your day, with an unrivalled personal touch and extraordinarily friendly service.

Please contact the restaurant for prices and details.

Other Recommended Hotels and Possible Reception Venues

Villa Maria ★ ★ ★ ★ www.villamaria.it	**Villa San Michele ★ ★** www.hotel-villasanmichele.it
Hotel Bonadies ★ ★ ★ ★ www.hotelbonadies.it	**Ristorante Cumpa Cosimo** Phone 089 857156
Hotel Toro ★ ★ ★ www.hoteltoro.it	**Ristorante Palazzo della Marra** www.palazzodellamarra.com/en/lecamere.asp
Hotel Parsifal ★ ★ ★ www.hotelparsifal.com	**Ristorante Vittoria** Phone 089 857947

How to Get There

From Naples International Airport

By car: Please note that cars are not permitted in Ravello town centre, and there are no parking facilities. However if you opt to drive, take the Naples – Pompeii – Salerno road and exit at Angri. Follow directions to "Valico di Chiunzi" and "Costiera Amalfitana". This will take you through the pass into Ravello. Distance from Naples is approximately 65km and takes around an hour.

Alternatively exit the road from Naples at Vietri Sul Mare and follow the Costiera Amalfitana towards Ravello, going through Cetara, Maori and Minori. Detailed routes can be found on www.autostrade.it/en/index.html.

By bus: To get to Ravello, you first need to get to Amalfi (see page 68). SITA buses run from Amalfi to Ravello's Piazza Vescovado (outside the *duomo*) around 15 times a day, and takes roughly half an hour.

SITA bus timetables can be found at www.sitabus.it/wps/portal/OrariCampania

Off the Beaten Track

Of course there are many places along the Amalfi Coast where you won't find glitz or glamour, and are well worth some investigation for that fact alone. Charming and unpretentious, these little villages and towns have a quiet, unspoilt rural beauty, that can be found just around the corner from the heaving tourist crowds (while feeling a million miles away) and where the locals actually treat Italian as their first language.

The first is **Praiano**, just east of Positano. Situated in a rock cleft and much smaller than its famous neighbour, it's still just about as expensive but much less crowded, especially in summer. Local co-ordinators are your best-placed resource if you're tempted to arrange a wedding here. A private boat tour of the nearby Grotta dello Smeraldo offers a great diversion for your guests.

Atrani is so close to Amalfi that it's more of an extension than a neighbour, albeit one that benefits from the proximity. Amalfi is such a draw that Atrani is largely ignored by the crowds, with the result that you can hold your wedding in a quiet, peaceful location while taking advantage of being a stone's throw from the biggest town in the area. Atrani has a pretty enclosed square and a large, domed Byzantine Church, the Church of San Salvatore. It's also one of the only towns in the area with a sandy beach.

The smallest of the Amalfi Coast towns is **Scala**. Situated right next to Ravello, it is a very peaceful, mountain town with the obligatory cathedral (Duomo San Lorenzo) and provides a real rural escape.

The hill town of **Minori** does experience some tourists, but it's still relatively undiscovered and is a pretty location. Its neighbour, **Maiori**, is a bigger town, although more modern and somehow not quite so romantic. Also nearby is the tiny fishing village of **Cetara** and the pretty town of **Vietri sul Mare**.

Local Information

Area Statistics for the Naples Region

	Ave. Sun (hrs)	Average Temperature Min	Average Temperature Max	Heat & Humidity	Average precipitation (mm)	Wet days	Sunset times Start of month	Sunset times End of month
Jan	4	4	12	-	116	11	17.46	17.19
Feb	4	5	13	-	85	10	17.20	17.52
March	5	6	15	-	73	9	17.54	19.26
April	7	9	18	-	62	8	19.27	19.58
May	8	12	22	-	44	7	19.59	20.27
June	9	16	26	Moderate	31	4	20.28	20.39
July	10	18	29	Medium	19	2	20.38	20.20
August	10	18	29	Medium	32	3	20.19	19.38
Sept	8	16	26	Moderate	64	5	19.36	18.48
Oct	6	12	22	-	107	9	18.46	17.01
Nov	4	9	17	-	147	11	17.00	16.36
Dec	3	6	14	-	135	12	16.36	16.45

Based on BBC weather statistics for Naples

Public Holidays	
January	1st – New Year's Day 6th – Epiphany
March April	Easter Weekend (date depending on year)
May	1st – Labour Day
June	2nd – Anniversary of the Republic
August	15th – Assumption of the Virgin
September	19th – San Gennaro
November	1st – All Saints' Day
December	8th – Day of the Immaculate Conception 25th – Christmas Day 26th – Boxing Day

Tourist Links

Vesuvius: www.laportadelvesuvio.it

Pompeii: www.pompeiisites.org

Boat Tours: www.alilauro.it, www.caremar.it, www.traghettipozzuoli.it

Tourist Information Links:
http://info.sorrentohelp.com
www.visitsorrento.com
www.sorrentotourism.com
www.virtualsorrento.com
www.sorrento-online.com
www.santagnello.info
www.positano.com
www.amalfi.it
www.amalficoastweb.com
www.comune.ravello.sa.it

White Pages

What follows is a variety of wedding-related suppliers based on the Amalfi Coast. These have been taken either from personal recommendations or from local company directories.

Do bear in mind that some of the smaller companies (hairdressers and florists in particular) are unlikely to speak much English so it would be advantageous to book through a co-ordinator rather than tackling them directly, unless you are fluent in Italian.

To conduct your own supplier searches, you can use online resources such as the Italian Yellow Pages, www.paginegialle.it/index.html, by entering the supplier type in *"Cosa"*, and the location in *"Dove"*.

Town Halls/Comuni

Naples Prefettura
Ufficio Legalizzazioni
Via Vespucci, 172
Napoli
Tel: +39 081 690 7337

Sorrento Town Hall
14, Piazza Sant'Antonino
80067 Sorrento (NA)
Tel: +39 081 533 5300
Fax: +39 081 533 5240
www.comuni-italiani.it/063/080/amm.html

Sant'agnello Town Hall
24, Piazza Matteotti
80065 Sant'agnello (NA)
Tel: +39 081 533 2111
Fax: +39 081 877 1226
www.comuni-italiani.it/063/071/amm.html

Positano Town Hall
111, Via G. Marconi
84017 Positano (SA)
Tel: +39 089 812 2511
Fax: +39 089 811 122
www.comuni-italiani.it/065/100/amm.html
www.comunedipositano.it/it/default.asp

Amalfi Town Hall
5, Piazza Municipio
84011 Amalfi (SA)
Tel: +39 089 873 6211
Fax: +39 089 871 646
www.comuni-italiani.it/065/006/amm.html

Ravello Town Hall
1, Via San Giovanni del Toro
84010 Ravello (SA)
Tel: +39 089 857 122
Fax: +39 089 857 185
www.comuni-italiani.it/065/104/amm.html

Minori Town Hall
Piazza G. Cantilena
84010 Minori (SA)
Tel: +39 089 877 135
Fax: +39 089 852 875
www.comuni-italiani.it/065/068/amm.html

Maiori Town Hall
71, Corso Reginna
84010 Maiori (SA)
Tel: +39 089 814 201
Fax: +39 089 853 133
www.comuni-italiani.it/065/066/amm.html

Atrani Town Hall
Via dei Dogi
84010 Atrini (SA)
Tel: +39 089 871 185
Fax: +39 089 871 484
www.comuni-italiani.it/065/011/amm.html

Praiano Town Hall
Via Umberto I
84010 Praiano (SA)
Tel: +39 089 874 026
Fax: +39 089 874 944
www.comuni-italiani.it/065/102/amm.html

Churches/Chiesa

Positano Cathedral
Chiesa di Santa Maria Assunta 1, Piazza Flavio Gioia 84017 Positano (SA) Tel: +39 089 812 129

Amalfi Cathedral
Duomo di Sant' Andrea Piazza del Duomo 84011 Amalfi (SA) Tel: +39 089 871 059

San Pietro Chapel
Capella di San Pietro Via Laurito 84017 Positano

Ravello Cathedral
Duomo di San Pantaleone Piazza Duomo 84010 Ravello Tel: +39 089 857 160 Fax: +39 178 603 9921 www.chiesaravello.com

Church of Santa Maria a Gradillo
Chiesa di Santa Maria a Gradillo 84017 Ravello

Featured Reception Venues

Sorrento

Grand Hotel Excelsior Vittoria
Piazza Tasso, 34
80067 Sorrento (NA)
Tel: +39 081 807 1044
Fax: +39 081 877 1206
www.exvitt.it

Hotel Bellevue Syrene
Piazza Vittoria, 5
80067 Sorrento (NA)
Tel: +39 081 878 1024
Fax: +39 081 878 3963
www.bellevue.it

Grand Hotel Royal
Via Correale, 42
PO Box 83
80067 Sorrento (NA)
Tel: +39 081 807 3434
Fax: +39 081 877 2905
www.royalsorrento.com

Ristorante O'Parrucchiano
Corso Italia, 71
80067 Sorrento (NA)
Tel: +39 081 878 1321
Fax: +39 081 532 4035
www.parrucchiano.com

Ristorante S. Antonino
Via S. Maria delle Grazie, 6
80067 Sorrento (NA)
www.weddingsorrento.it

Photo Food & Drinks
Via Correale, 19
80067 Sorrento (NA)
Tel: +39 081 877 3686
www.photosorrento.com

Positano

Hotel Covo dei Saraceni
Via Regina Giovanna, 5
84017 Positano (SA)
Tel: +39 089 875 400
Fax: +39 089 875 878
www.covodeisaraceni.com

Hotel Palazzo Murat
Via dei Mulini, 23
84017 Positano (SA)
Tel: +39 089 875 177
Fax: +39 089 811 419
www.palazzomurat.it

Hotel Conca d'Oro
Via Boscariello, 16
84017 Positano (SA)
Tel: +39 089 875 111
Fax: +39 089 811 494
www.hotel-concadoro.com

Ristorante Le Terrazze
Via Grotte dell'Incanto, 51
84017 Positano (SA)
Tel: +39 089 875 874
Fax: +39 089 812 2807
www.leterrazzarestaurant.it

Amalfi

Hotel Santa Caterina
84011 Amalfi (SA)
Tel: +39 089 871 012
Fax: +39 089 871 351
www.hotelsantacaterina.it

Hotel Luna Convento
Via P. Comite
84011 Amalfi (SA)
Tel: +39 089 871 002
Fax: +39 089 871 050
www.lunahotel.it

Ristorante EOLO
Via P. Comite, 19
84011 Amalfi (SA)
Tel: +39 089 871 104
Fax: +39 089 871 024
www.marinariviera.it/eolo

Ravello
Hotel Caruso Piazza San Giovanni del Toro, 2 84010 Ravello (SA) Tel: +39 089 858 801 Fax: +39 089 858 806 www.hotelcaruso.com **Hotel Palumbo** Via San Giovanni del Toro 84010 Ravello (SA) Tel: +39 089 857 244 www.hotelpalumbo.it **Villa Cimbrone** Via S. Chiara, 26 84010 Ravello (SA) Tel: +39 089 857 459 Fax: +39 089 857 777 www.villacimbrone.com **Mamma Agata** Piazza S. Cosma, 9 84010 Ravello (SA) Tel: +39 089 857 019 Fax: +39 089 858 432 www.mammaagata.com **Hotel Ristorante Garden** Via Boccaccio, 4 84010 Ravello (SA) Tel: +39 089 857 726 Fax: +39 089 858 110 www.hotelgardenravello.it

Wedding Co-ordinators & Tour Operators

Sorrento
The Book of Dreams
Tel: +39 081 532 1223
Email: info@thebookofdreams.net
Web: www.thebookofdreams.net
Highly Recommended

Sorrento Weddings
2, Largo S. Francesco
80067 Sorrento (NA)
Tel: +39 081 807 4406
Fax. +39 081 8774187
Email: info@palazzomarziale.com
Web: www.sorrentoweddings.net

Wedding & Joy
Sorrento
Tel: +39 335 546 4321
Email: info@weddingandjoy.com
Web: www.weddingandjoy.com

Tour Operators serving Sorrento:
Citalia, Cosmos, Cresta, First Choice, Kirker, Kuoni, Magic of Italy, Thomas Cook, Thomson, Top Level Travel

Amalfi
Amalfi Weddings
Email: weddings@amalfi-weddings.com
Web: www.amalfi-weddings.com

Amalfi Life
1, Via Corte
84011 Amalfi (SA)
Tel: +39 089 813 028
Email: laurie@amalfilife.com
Web: www.amalfilife.com

Tour Operators serving Amalfi:
Citalia, Kuoni, Magic of Italy, Thomson

Atrani
La Calla
3/5, Corso Vittorio Emanuele
84010 Atrani (SA)
Tel: +39 089 873551
Fax: +39 089 8304107
Email: info@lacalla.it
Web: www.lacalla.it/english/default.asp
Highly Recommended

Ravello
Ravello Events
3, Via Roma
84010 Ravello (SA)
Tel: +39 089 8586272
Fax: +39 089 8586443
Email: info@ravelloevents.com
Web: www.ravelloevents.com/english.asp

Tour Operators serving Ravello:
Citalia, Magic of Italy, Thomson

Minori
Amalfi Coast Wedding
3, Via Monte
84010 Minori
Tel: +39 329 214 9811
Email: info@weddingamalficoast.com
Web: www.weddingamalficoast.com

Tour Operators serving Minori:
Thomson

Positano
Positano Luxury Events S.r.l.
247, Via Pasitea
Positano (SA)
Email: info@positanoluxuryevents.it
Web: www.positanoluxuryevents.it/ing/positanowedding/default.asp

Tour Operators serving Positano:
Citalia, Kirker, Magic of Italy, Thomson

Tour Operators serving Sant'agnello:
Magic of Italy, Thomas Cook, Citalia

Tour Operators serving Piano di Sorrento:
First Choice, Thomson

Tour Operators serving Maiori:
Thomson

Tour Operators serving Meta:
Thomson

Independent Translator

Regional
Carmela Cesarano
Tel: +39 348 713 6590
Email: carmela.cesarano@hotmail.it

Photographers & Videographers / Fotografo

Sorrento & Sant'Agnello

Videomania Creativestudio
Marrazzo Fabio
Via S. Maria Pieta', 16
80067 Sorrento (NA)
Tel: +39 081 877 0679
www.videomania.tv
Recommended

Gargiulo Michele Fotografi
Vicolo San Cesareo I, 4
80067 Sorrento (NA)
Tel: +39 081 878 2022

Gargiulo Antonino Fotosport
Via Vittorio Veneto, 12
80067 Sorrento (NA)
Tel: +39 081 878 1188

Iride Service di Berrino M.E.C. S.A.S Laboratorio Fotografico
Via Fuori Mura, 20
80067 Sorrento (NA)
Tel: +39 081 877 2670

Fotografare di Soldatini L.
Via Fuoro
80067 Sorrento (NA)
Tel: +39 081 807 3243

FA GI Video
Fattorusso Giuseppe
Via Degli Aranci, 130
Sorrento (NA)
Tel: +39 081 8785941
http://www.sorrentosposi.it/fagivideo.html

Valerio Gargiulo
Corso Italia, 258/B
Sorrento (NA)

Fotocenter di Coluccino Tiziana E Giuseppe Snc
27/C, Corso Italia
80065 Sant'agnello (NA)
Tel: +39 081 878 1889

Puoti Raffaele Studio Laboratorio Fotografico
26, Via Cappuccini
80065 Sant'agnello (NA)
Tel: +39 081 878 5744

Piano di Sorrento

Photo 105
Giuseppe Coppola
Via Bagnulo, 38
Piano di Sorrento (NA)
Tel. +39 081 5321346

Positano

Mascolo Raffaele Nuova Fotografia
12, Via C. Colombo
84017 Positano (SA)
Tel: +39 089 811018

Foto Nuova Fotografia
Alfonso Fusco
Tel: +39 089 875644

Amalfi

A&5 Photo Studio
29, Via Lorenzo d'Amalfi
84011 Amalfi (SA)
Tel: +39 089 872410

Gambardella Rag. Nicola Studio d'Arte Fotografica
8, Piazza Municipio
84011 Amalfi (SA)
Tel: +39 089 871082

Ravello

Foto Maniglia
22, Via P.Co Della Rimembranza
84010 Ravello (SA)
Tel: +39 089 857336

Regional

JoAnne Dunn Photographer
47b, Via del Monte
84012 Angri (SA)
Tel: +39 081 947413
Email: info@joannedunn.it
Web: www.joannedunn.it
Highly Recommended

Angelo Oliva
Via Ferreria, 44
Baronisi (SA)
Tel: +39 089 956 5224
Email: info@angelolivia.it
Web: www.angeloliva.it

Alfonso Longobardi
Via Satriano coop A. Moro
Angri (SA)
Tel: 0161 421 0005 (UK)
Email: carmen@alfonsolongobardi.com
Web: www.field.it

Giuseppe di Maio
Tel: +39 089 865179
Email: giuseppedimaiofotografo@hotmail.it
Web: www.giuseppedimaio.it

Foto Smeraldo
Ingenito Luigi
Via Filangieri, 53
Vico Equense (NA)

Maga Video
Gargiulo Mario
Via Roncato, 5
Massa Lubrense (NA)

Salvir Cine-Foto-Video
Via Severo Caputo, 8
Monticchio (NA)

Ladies' Hairdressers / Parrucchieri

Sorrento

Beauty Line di Esposito Luisa
Via Degli Aranci, 9
80067 Sorrento (NA)
Tel: +39 081 807 2515
Highly Recommended

Antoine's
Via Luigi de Maio
80067 Sorrento (NA)
Highly Recommended

Gianni Coiffeur di Rosario Canonico E C. Snc Parucchiere per Signora
Piazza S. Antonio, 15
80067 Sorrento (NA)
Tel: +39 081 878 2515

Esposito Antonina Parr. Per Signora
Via de Maio Luigi, 8
80067 Sorrento (NA)
Tel: +39 081 878 2753

Parrucchiere Glamour do Fruscio Antonio Centro de Bellezza
Via De Maio Luigi, 27
80067 Sorrento (NA)
Tel: +39 081 878 4158

Efetto Donna Di Caso G.
Via Tasso Torquato, 34
80067 Sorrento (NA)
Tel: +39 081 807 4430

Peppino & Mirella Parrucchiere per Signora
Via Vittorio Veneto, 8/10
80067 Sorrento (NA)
Tel: +39 081 877 1180

De Gregorio Giuseppe Coiffeur pour Dames
Via Degli Aranci, 27/B
80067 Sorrento (NA)
Tel: +39 081 878 2548

De Rosa Parrucchiere per Signora
Piazza Lauro Angelina, 43
80067 Sorrento (NA)
Tel: +39 081 878 4965

D'esposito Giulio
Piazza A. Lauro, 33
80067 Sorrento (NA)

Evolution Hair
Vico II fuoro, 13
80067 Sorrento (NA)
Tel. +39 081 8771507

Parrucchiere Glamour
Via Luigi De Maio, 27
80067 Sorrento (NA)

Piano di Sorrento

D'Arco Francesco Paolo Parruchier Per Signora
Corso Italia, 245
80063 Piano Di Sorrento (NA)
Tel: +39 081 532 3191

Di Donna Gaetano Parrucchiere Per Signora
Corso Italia
80063 Piano Di Sorrento (NA)
Tel: +39 081 878 8463

Massa Francsco L'Altro Mondo Studio
Corso Italia, 169
80063 Piano Di Sorrento (NA)
Tel: +39 081 878 8584

Mauri & Max Hair Styling Snc Di Massimo E Maurizio Scognamiglio
Corso Italia, 197
80063 Piano Di Sorrento (NA)
Tel: +39 081 532 1047

Parrucchiere Bianca Di Vicentini B.
Corso Italia, 335
80063 Piano Di Sorrento (NA)
Tel: +39 081 808 6404

Pepino & Mirella Di Abbisogno Giuseppe E Parlato Sivia Snc
Corso Italia, 138
80063 Piano Di Sorrento (NA)
Tel: +39 081 808 7248

Vanity Hair Snc
Via Italia, 369
80063 Piano Di Sorrento (NA)
Tel: +39 081 532 1271

Linea Donna
Via delle Rose, 31
Piano di Sorrento (NA)

Meta
Fashion Point
Via Angelo Cosenza, 15
Meta (NA)

Sant'Agnello
Federico Bruna Stella Acconciature Per Signora
Corso Italia, 200
80065 Sant'agnello (NA)
Tel: +39 081 532 1257

Parrucchiere Per Signora' Adriana'
Corso Italia, 90
80065 Sant'agnello (NA)
Tel: +39 081 878 2440

Positano
Della Mura Patrizia Parrucchiere
Via Leucosia, 3
84017 Positano (SA)
Tel: +39 089 875447

Color Fashion Di Avitabile Enrico
Via Pasitea, 213
84017 Positano (SA)
Tel: +39 089 812075

D'Urso Rosa Uomo Donna Estetica
Via Pasitea
84017 Positano (SA)
Tel: +39 089 875315

Dacci Un Taglio S.A.S. Di De Martino Andrea & Co
Via Pasitea, 242
84017 Positano (SA)
Tel: +39 089 811184

Graziella Linea Coiffeur
Via Pasitea, 1/2
84017 Positano (SA)
Tel: +39 089 875976

Luisa E Flavia Coiffeur
Tel: +39 089 875447

Ravello
Serretiello Aldo Parrucchiere
Via Dei Rufolo, 18
84010 Ravello (SA)
Tel: +39 089 857117

Lello Parrucchiere Per Signora
Via Boccaccio, 7
84010 Ravello (SA)
Tel: +39 089 857300

Maresca Davide Coiffeur
Parco Della Rimembranza, 31
84010 Ravello (SA)
Tel: +39 089 858300

Lucibello Francesca Parrucchiera
Via Lacco, 13
84010 Ravello (SA)
Tel: +39 089 857029

Beauticians / Estetista

Sorrento

Beauty Line di Esposito Luisa
Via Degli Aranci, 9
80067 Sorrento (NA)
Tel: +39 081 807 2515
Highly Recommended

Estetista Rita Gargiulo Trattamenti Curativi
Via Degli Aranci, 33
80067 Sorrento (NA)
Tel: +39 081 878 2497

Centro Donna S.A.S.
Via Degli Aranci, 11
80067 Sorrento (NA)

Phitoestetica Pagard
Corso Italia, 263/b
80067 Sorrento (NA)

Studio Estetica
Corso Italia, 38
80067 Sorrento (NA)

Amalfi

Torre Patrizia Estetista
Via E. Marini, 10
84011 Amalfi (SA)
Tel: +39 089 872545

Mediterranea S.A.S. Di Sonia Capone Beauty & Relax
Via P. Capuano, 4
84011 Amalfi (SA)
Tel: +39 089 873594

Ersilia Estetista E Pedicure Curativa
Via Roma, 35
84011 Amalfi (SA)
Tel: +39 089 871327

Piano di Sorrento

Eversun Club Di Esposito I. E Somma C. S.N.C.
Corso Italia
80063 Piano di Sorrento (NA)
Tel: +39 081 534 1136

Kama - Kura Estetica
Corso Italia, 238
80063 Piano di Sorrento
Tel: +39 081 808 7678

Idea Bellezza
Corso Italia, 216
80063 Piano di Sorrento (NA)

Instituto di Bellezza Elle
Corso Italia, 84
80063 Piano di Sorrento (NA)

Kama Kura
Corso Italia, 238
80063 Piano di Sorrento (NA)

Sant'agnello

Centro Estetico Naturopatico Lorimatico Sas Di Loguercio Lorella
Via S. Martino, 11
80065 Sant'agnello (NA)
Tel: +39 081 878 4413

Lady Estetica Instituto Bellezza
Via A. Balsamo, 35
80065 Sant'Agnello (NA)

Men's Hairdressers / Parrucchieri per Uomo, Barbieri

Sorrento
Bonaparte Hair Stylist for Men Acconciature Manicure Pedicure Piazza Tasso Torquato 80067 Sorrento (NA) Tel: +39 081 878 4320 **Janvier di Amitrano Gennaro Parrucchiere Per Signore** 10, Via Fuori Mura 80067 Sorrento (NA) Tel: +39 081 807 1988 **Agrillo Antonino Parrucchiere per Uomo (also for wet shaves)** 39, Via Fuoro 80067 Sorrento (NA) Tel: +39 081 877 1612 **Brupinsal Parruccheiere Uomo** 289, Corso Italia 80067 Sorrento (NA) Tel: +39 081 878 4201 **Esposito Andrea** 319/A, Corso Italia 80067 Sorrento (NA) Tel: +39 081 807 4706 **Miccio Antonio Acconciature Aschili** 4, Via Atigliana 80067 Sorrento (NA) Tel: +39 081 878 4617

Piano di Sorrento
De Martino Francesco 115, Corso Italia 80063 Piano Di Sorrento (NA) Tel: +39 081 532 1952 **Pollio Michele Acconciature Maschili** 21, Via Ripa Di Cassano 80063 Piano di Sorrento (NA) Tel: +39 081 878 6491

Positano
D'Urso Rosa Uomo Donna Estetica Via Pasitea 84017 Positano (SA) Tel: +39 089 875315 **Dacci Un Taglio S.A.S. Di De Martino Andrea & Co** 242, Via Pasitea 84017 Positano (SA) Tel: +39 089 811184

Amalfi
Serretiello Renato Parrucchiere Per Uomo 21, Via Roma 84011 Amalfi (SA) Tel: +39 089 871206

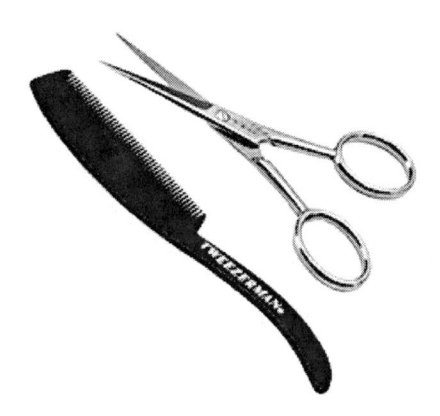

Florists / Fioraio

Sorrento

**Superflora
(Di Aversa Rosa E C. S.N.C.)**
2, Via S. Francesco
80067 Sorrento (NA)
Tel: +39 081 878 2555
Tel: +39 081 807 1096
Highly Recommended

Terrecuso Giuseppe Fiori
44, Via S. Cesareo
80067 Sorrento (NA)
Tel: +39 081 878 3941

Fasulo Olga Fiori E Piante
18, Piazza Tasso Torquato,
80067 Sorrento (NA)
Tel: +39 081 878 1263

Pontecorvo Sabato Il Nido Dei Fiori
9, Vicolo Il Fuoro
80067 Sorrento (NA)
Tel: +39 081 807 1385

Amalfi

Posa Flora
Via Mauro Comite
Biveo per Agerola
Amalfi
Tel: +39 089 831833
Email: info@posaflora.it
Web: www.posaflora.it

Torre Guido Fioraio
2, Via Pietro Capuano
84011 Amalfi (SA)
Tel: +39 089 872362

Ceruleo Maria
26, Piazza Spirito Santo
84011 Amalfi (SA)
Tel: +39 089 872971

Ceruleo Bonaventura
1, Via Pantaleone Comite
84011 Amalfi (SA)
Tel: +39 089 871494

Piano di Sorrento

Aiello Giancarlo Fioraio
169, Corso Italia
80063 Piano di Sorrento (NA)
Tel: +39 081 878 7491

Iaccarino Pasquale
213, Corso Italia
80063 Piano di Sorrento (NA)
Tel: +39 081 878 6182

Sant'agnello

Gargiulo Giuseppe Fiori E Piante
63, Corso Italia
80065 Sant'agnello (NA)
Tel: +39 081 878 3646

Starita Giuseppe
83, Corso Italia
80065 Sant'agnello (NA)
Tel: +39 081 878 4691

Ferraiuolo Fiori - Piante - Addobbi
9, Via Crawford
80065 Sant'agnello (NA)
Tel: +39 081 878 5923

Positano

Posa Flora
Via G. Marconi, 260
Positano
Tel: +39 089 811668
Email: info@posaflora.it
Web: www.posaflora.it

Flora Gardelaldo
Via G. Marconi, 270
Positano
Tel: +39 089 812 3248
Email: info@floragardenaldo.it
Web: www.floragardenaldo.it

Positan Flower di Rianna Antonino
51, Via Pasitea
84017 Positano (SA)
Tel: +39 089 875327

Ravello

Malafronte Armando & C. Sas Fiori E Piante
19, Via Roma
84010 Ravello (SA)
Tel: +39 089 857767
http://www.malafronte.com/

Transportation

Wedding Day Cars & Limos / Auto da Ceremonia

Sorrento

Autonoleggio Sorrento S.r.l.
Corso Italia 210 /A
Sorrento (NA)
Tel. +39 081 8781386
Fax. +39 081 8785039
Web:
www.sorrento.it/english_version/index.htm

Austoservizi De Martino
Also offers private yachts
Via degli Aranci, 29/E
Via Parsano, 8
Corso Italia, 253
80067 Sorrento (NA)
Tel. 081.8782801 - Fax 081.8071013
Web: www.autoservizidemartio.com/auto_services_sorrento.asp

Piccola Coop. Sorrento
Via Marziale 45/b
Vico I Fuoro 4
80067 Sorrento (NA)
Tel +39.0818075895
Fax +39.0815324623
E-mail: info@piccolacooperativasorrento.com
Web:
www.piccolacooperativasorrento.com/english/index.html

Jolly Servizi
180, Via Degli Aranci
29, Via Fuorimura
80067 Sorrento (NA)
Tel: +39 081 977 3450
Tel: +39 081 878 1719
Fax: +39 081 877 1999
Web:
www.jollyservizi.it/english/services.htm

Sant'agnello

Caruso Limo
Corsa Italia 167
80065 Sant'agnello (NA)
Tel: +39 081 532 2247
Fax: +39 081 532 3610
Info@carusolimo.com
www.carusolimo.com

Positano

Benvenuto Chauffeur Services
54, Via Roma
84010 Praiano (SA)
Tel: +39 334 307 8342
Web: www.benvenutolimos.com
Email: info@benvenutolimos.com

Limousine Service
111, Via Pasitea
84017 Positano (SA)
Tel: +39 089 811 624
Fax: +39 089 875 485
Web:
www.limocarservice.net/english/lastoria.htm

Scooters / Motorina

Sorrento

Happy Rent
Corso Italia, 257
Sorrento (NA)
Tel. +39 081 877 4664

Sorrento Rent a Scooter
Corso Italia, 210
Sorrento (NA)
Tel. +39 081 878 1386

Positano

Positano Rent a Scooter
Via Pasitea, 99
84017 Positano (SA)
Tel. +39 089 812 2077
www.positanorentascooter.com

Bakeries / Panetteria

Sorrento
De Palmo Maurizio Snc Panificio Biscottificio Via Fuoro, 40 80067 Sorrento (NA) Tel: +39 081 807 3506

Amalfi
Vecchio Mulino di Bellogrado Antonio & C. Snc Panificio Vecchio 28, Via P. Capuano 84011 Amalfi (SA) Tel: +39 089 871400
Panificio Erasmo Pacileo Di Pacileo & C. Panificio 7, Piazza Dei Dogi 84011 Amalfi (SA) Tel: +39 089 873377
Vecchio Mulino Di Bellogrado Antonio & C. S.N.C. Panetteria 94, Via Delle Cartiere 84011 Amalfi (SA) Tel: +39 089 872185

Piano di Sorrento
Panificio Ercolano Snc Ercorlano Gaetano Via Delle Rose 80063 Piano di Sorrento (NA) Tel: +39 081 878 6222
Sfizi Di Pane Di Puca Raffaella 9, Via Ciampa Francesco 80063 Piano di Sorrento (NA) Tel: +39 081 808 7804

Sant'agnello
Russo Giuseppina Vendita Pane 7, Via Cimitero 80065 Sant'agnello (NA) Tel: 081 877 2645

Positano
Forno Delle Gr. Di Crisculo Via Mons Vito Talamo, 47 84017 Positano (SA) Tel: +39 089 811 464

Favours / Bomboniere & Confezioni

Sorrento
Aiello Michele 44, Strada Fuoro 80067 Sorrento (NA) Atelier della Bomboniera - Sharon 259/a, Corso Italia 80067 Sorrento (NA) Gabriella di Fiorentino Emilio 10, Str. Tasso 80067 Sorrento (NA)

Piano di Sorrento
Emilsose 155, Corso Italia 80063 Piano di Sorrento (NA)

Musicians / Musicisti

Musica Eventi
7, Parco S. Paolo is. 80126 Napoli (I) Phone: +39 081 658 3136 Web: www.musicaeventi.it

Armonia
88, Via P. Castellino Napoli Email: info@armoniaweb.it Web: www.armoniaweb.it

DJ Planet Di Capone Giuseppe Disco Import
152, Corso Reginna 84010 Maiori (SA) Tel: +39 089 852377

Wedding Apparel / Abiti per Ceremonia

Sorrento
Boutique Mario - Uomo 128, Corso Italia 212, Corso Italia Sorrento (NA) Tel: +39 81 878 1361 Fax: +39 81 592 4889 Web: www.marioadario.it **Cherie Moda Sposa S.R.L.** 40, Via Correale Sorrento (NA) Tel: 081 801 878 1649 Web: www.cheriemodasposa.it

Sant'agnello
Grazia Sposa 2, Via Crawford 80065 Sant'agnello (NA) Tel: +39 081 877 3968 Web: www.graziasposa.com

Regional
Angelina Abbigliamento Corso Italia, 28 Meta (NA) **Cherie Mode Boutique** Via S.Ciro, 3 Vico Equense (NA) **Liabella** C.so Italia, 65/69 Piano di Sorrento (NA)

Bibliography

Belford, Ros; Dunford, M; Woolfrey, C. *The Rough Guide to Italy.* London, England: Rough Guides, 2005.

Copeman-Bryant, Callie. *A Marriage Made in Italy: The Wedding Planning Guide.* Cambridge, England: A Marriage Made Publications, 2006.

Facaros, D; Pauls, M. *Bay of Naples & Southern Italy.* London, England: Cadogan Guides, 2005

Francesio, G. *Naples & The Amalfi Coast.* London, England: Dorling Kindersley Ltd, 1997.

Garwood, G; Quintero, J. *Naples & the Amalfi Coast.* London, England: Lonely Planet Publications Pty Ltd, 2006

Podesta, Gina. *A Romantic's Guide to Italy.* Berkeley, Canada: Ten Speed Press, 2004.

Online Sources
www.bbc.co.uk
www.britishembassy.gov.uk
www.clickbridal.com
www.comuni-italiani.it
www.confetti.co.uk
www.embitaly.org.uk
www.fco.gov.uk
www.fepqep.org
www.hitched.co.uk
www.imdb.com
www.intoitaly.it
www.italiansrus.com
www.italiantourism.com
www.italiantouristboard.co.uk
www.italyheaven.co.uk
www.italy-weddings.com
www.itconlond.org.uk
www.paginegialle.it
http://roma.katolsk.no/index.htm
www.siafitalia.org
www.sposi.it
www.theknot.com
www.tripadvisor.co.uk
www.vicariatusurbis.org/
www.virtualitalia.com
www.weddingchaos.co.uk
www.weddingguide.co.uk
www.weddings-abroad-guide.com
www.weddingsonline.ie

Acknowledgements

I would like to thank the following people for their assistance in helping me put this work together: Positano Town hall for all the fantastic information, all the hotels featured for their patience, help and professionalism; JoAnne Dunn and Camilla Cesarano for allowing me to use the wonderful photographs; the message board participants of Hitched, Confetti, Wedding Guide, The Knot, The Weddings Abroad Guide and Weddings Online and all the brides who have bombarded me with emails to tell me about their frustrations and give me plenty of ideas.

I'd also like to thank my husband James for making all those research trips far more romantic than they would otherwise have been. *Tu sei una stella!*

©JoAnne Dunn Photographer

Index

airlines, 4
airports, 4, 31, 32, 51, 68, 89
Angri, 89
Amalfi, **52-68**
Amalfi Cathedral, 52, 54, **59-60**, 95
Amalfi Coast Drive, 4, 34, 52, 69, 90
Amalfi Town Hall. See *Salone Morelli*
A Marriage Made in Italy – The Wedding Planning Guide, 5, 12, 38, 55, 73
anagrafe. See *Town Hall*
Anglican ceremonies, 12, 64, 78, 81
Archdiocese of Salerno, 12
Archdiocese of Sorrento/CastelImmare, 12
Atrani, 53, 90
Atrani Town Hall, 94
bakeries, 109
bands, 110
banns, 12
barbers. See *men's hairdressers*
Bay of Naples, 3, 17, 20, 22
Bay of Salerno, 3, 52
beach, 43, 44, 90
beauticians, 104
bibliography, 112
boats. See *ferries*
bolli, 12, 38, 55, 73
bomboniere, 109
buses, 31, 51, 68, 89
Capri, 12, 53, 68
cars/car hire, 32, 51, 68, 89, 108
Casa Albertina, 50
Catholic ceremonies, 13, 55, 59, 64
Catholic churches, 12, 42-43, 59-60, 64, 76-77, 95
Certificate of No Impediment. See *Nulla Osta*
Cetara, 90
Chapel at Hotel Luna Convento, 63
Chapel of San Pietro, 36, **42**, 95
Christmas, 91
churches. See *Catholic Churches*
Circumvesuviana, 32, 33
civil ceremonies, 12, 13-17, 40, 55, 57, 73, 74
civil venues, 13-17, 40-41, 57-58, 74-75
climate, 4, 91
Cloisters of the Church of San Francesco, 10, 11, *13*, **14-15**, 16
Comune, 12, 38, 40, 55, 73, 74, 94
consular office, 6
Convent of Santa Maria delle Grazie, 10, 11, **16**
cooking school, 86
costs, 5
co-ordinator. See *wedding co-ordinator*
Curreri Bus Service. See *buses*
declaration to marry, 12, 38, 55, 73
deposits, 5
DH Lawrence, 78
discos, 27, 110
driving, 32, 51, 68, 89
documents, 12

Duomo di Sant Andreo. See *Amalfi Cathedral*
Duomo di Santa Maria Assunta. See *Positano Cathedral*
Easter, 4
Elizabeth Taylor, 86
Enrico Caruso, 19
favours, 109
ferries, 31, 51, 68
fireworks, 48
florist, 106-107
Fred Astaire, 86
Gore Vidal, 84
Grand Hotel Ambasciadori, 30
Grand Hotel Royal, 10, 11, **23**, 96
Greta Garbo, 78
hairdressers, 102-103. See also *men's hairdressers*
heat. See *climate*
hen nights, 49, 87
Hotel Albergo Miramare, 50
Hotel Alpha, 30
Hotel Amalfi, 67
Hotel Angelina, 30
Hotel Antica Repubblica Amalfi, 67
Hotel Antiche Mura, 30
Hotel Belair, 30
Hotel Bellevue Syrene, 10, 11, **21-22**, 96
Hotel Bonadies, 88
Hotel Buca di Bacco, 50
Hotel California, 50
Hotel Caravel, 30
Hotel Caruso Belvedere, 71, 72, **82-83**, 97
Hotel Centrale, 67
Hotel Christina, 30
Hotel Conca d'Oro, 36, 37, **47-48**, 96
Hotel Cocumella, 30
Hotel Covo dei Saraceni, 36, 37, **44-45**, 96
Hotel Eden Roc Suites, 50
Hotel Excelsior Vittoria, 10, 11, **19-20**, 96
Hotel Floridiana, 67
Hotel Fontana, 67
Hotel Il Nido, 30
Hotel La Pace, 30
Hotel La Pergola, 30
Hotel Lidomare, 67
Hotel Luna Convento, 54, **63-64**, 96
Hotel Marina Riviera, 54, **65-66**, 96
Hotel Marincanto, 50
Hotel Michelangelo, 30
Hotel Mignon, 30
Hotel Miramalfi, 67
Hotel Miramare, 50
Hotel Mediterraneo, 30
Hotel Minerva, 30
Hotel Nice, 30
Hotel Palazzo Murat, 36, 37, **46**, 96
Hotel Palumbo, 71, 72, **80-81**, 97
Hotel Parsifal, 88
Hotel Poseidon, 50
Hotel Pupetto, 50

Hotel Ristorante Garden, 71, 72, **84-85**, 97
Hotel Santa Caterina, 54, **61-70**, 96
Hotel Toro, 88
Hotel Tramontano, 30
Hotel Villa Franca, 50
Hotel Villa Lara, 67
Hotel Villa Maria, 88
Hotel Villa San Michele, 88
Humphrey Bogart, 63, 86
humidity. See *climate*
hydrofoils, 31
interpreter, 12, 38, 55, 73
Il Mirto Bianco, 30
Immigration Office, Naples. See *Preffetura*
Ingrid Bergman, 63
Ischia, 53, 68
Jewish ceremonies, 78
Lady Chatterley's Lover, 78
La Tonnarella, 30
legal requirements, 5, 6, 12, 38, 55, 73
lemon groves, 9, 61, 64
Lent, 4
limousines, 108
Littari Mountains, 81
Maiori, 90
Maiori Town Hall, 94
Mama Camilla, 30
Marilyn Monroe, 19
men's hairdressers, 105
Megellina Port, 31
Minori, 90
Minori Town Hall, 94
Modigliani, 80
Morelli, Dominico, 57
Music on the Rocks, **49**
musicians, 110
Naples Airport. See *airports*
Naples Immigration Office. See *Preffetura*
Naples Port, 31, 68
Napoli Centrali Station, 31
night club, 49
Nulla Osta, 12, 38, 55, 73
O'Parruchiano. See *Ristorante O'Parruchiano*
paperwork, 12, 38, 55, 73
Palazzo Tolla, 71, 72, **74-75**, 94
parking, 32, 51, 89
peak season, 4, 8, 17, 25, 39, 49, 52, 73
Pensione Maria Luisa, 50
photographer, 100-101
Photo Food & Drinks. See *Ristorante Photo Food & Drinks*
pianists. See *musicians*
Piano di Sorrento, 17
Piazza Flavio Gioia, 68
Piazza Garibaldi. See *Napoli Central Station*
Piazza Municipio, 31, 57
Piazza San'Antonino, 16
Piazza Tasso, 14, 20, 28, 31
Piazza Vescovado, 89
planner. See *wedding co-ordinator*
Tarantella, 22, 83

Pompeii, 92
Positano, **34-51**
Positano Cathedral, 36, **43**, 94
Positano Town Hall, 36, 37, 39, **40-41**, 47, 55, 94
Positano Wedding Balcony. See *Positano Town Hall*
Praiano, 53, 90
Praiano Town Hall, 94
Preffetura, 12, 94
price per head, 5
Protestant ceremonies, 78, 81
public holidays, 91
rainfall. See *climate*
Ravello, **69-89**
Ravello Cathedral, 71, 72, **76**, 89, 95
Ravello Town Hall. See *Palazzo Tolla*
religious ceremonies, 12, 38, 55, 73
religious venues. See *Catholic Churches*
Richard Burton, 86
Ristorante Cumpa Cosimo, 88
Ristorante EOLO, 54, **65-66**, 96
Ristorante Garden, 71, 72, **84-85**, 97
Ristorante La Caravalla, 67
Ristorante Le Terrazze, 36, 37, 49
Ristorante Mamma Agata, 71, 72, **86-87**, 97
Ristorante O'Parruchaino, 10, 11, **24-25**, 96
Ristorante Palazzo della Marra, 88
Ristorante Photo Food & Drinks, 10, 11, **28-29**, 96
Ristorante Sant'Antonino, 10, 11, **26-27**, 96
Ristorante Vittoria, 88
Rome International Airport, 32
Salerno, 68, 89
Salone Morelli, 54, **57-58**, 94
San Francesco Cloisters. See *Cloisters of the Church of San Francesco*
Sant'agnello, **9**
Sant'agnello Town Hall, 94
Santa Maria a Gradillo, 71, 72, **77**, 95
Santa Maria Assunta. See *Positano Cathedral*
Santa Maria delle Grazie Convent. See *Convent of Santa Maria delle Grazie*
Sant'Antonino. See *Ristorante Sant'Antonino*
Scala, 90
Scoppetta, Pietro, 57
scooters, 33, 108
Simone de Beauvoir, 63, 64
singers. See *musicians*
Sophia Loren, 19
Sorrento, 3, **7-8**, 12
Sorrento Civil Registrar. See *Ufficiale dello Statto Civile*
Sorrento Port, 31, 51, 68
Sorrento Town Hall, 94
stag nights, 49
sunrise times, 91
sunsets, 4, 91
sunset times, 91
symbolic ceremonies, 12, 78, 81
taxis, 31

temperatures. See *climate*
Tenessee Williams, 80
Top Pick Logo, 5
tour operator, 12, 38, 55, 73, 98, 99
tourist information, 92
tourists, 8, 9, 14, 59, 69, 73
Town Hall. See *Comune*
trains, 31
translator, 99
Ufficiale dello Stato Civile, 12
Ufficio Legalizzazioni. See *Preffetura*
videographer, 100, 101
venue hire, 5
Vesuvius, 4, 8, 17, 20
Via Vespucci. See *Preffetura*
Viale Pasitea, 51
Vietri sul Mare, 90
Villa Cimbrone, 71, 72, **78-79**, 97
Villa Fiorentina, 50
Villa Fondi, **17**
Villa Nettuno, 50
Villa Rufolo, 74, 84
Wagner, 80
Wedding Balcony. See *Positano Town Hall*
wedding cake, 5, 109
wedding co-ordinator, 12, 38, 39, 55, 73, 98-99
wedding dresses, 111
wedding planner. See *wedding co-ordinator*
White Pages, 93

Printed in the United Kingdom
by Lightning Source UK Ltd.
136281UK00001B/355/P